STEPHEN CRANE
A STUDY IN AMERICAN LETTERS

STEPHEN CRANE
IN ENGLAND

THOMAS BEER

STEPHEN CRANE

A STUDY IN AMERICAN LETTERS

With an Introduction by
JOSEPH CONRAD

GARDEN CITY, NEW YORK
GARDEN CITY PUBLISHING CO., INC.

R0736

For

ROBERT HOUSUM

CONTENTS

INTRODUCTION

On a rainy day of March of the year 1923, listening to the author of this biography telling me of his earnest labours for the memory of a man who was certainly unique in his generation I exclaimed to myself with wonder: "And so it has come to pass after all—this thing which I did not expect to see!" In truth I had never expected the biography of Stephen Crane to appear in my lifetime. My immense pleasure was affected by the devastating touch of time which like a muddy flood covers under a mass of daily trivialities things of value: moments of affectionate communion with kindred spirits, words spoken with the careless freedom of perfect confidence, the deepest emotions of joy and sorrow— together with such things of merely historical importance as the recollection of dates, for instance. After hearing from Mr. Beer of his difficulties in fixing certain dates in the history of Stephen Crane's life I discovered that I was unable to remember with any kind of precision the initial date of our friendship. Indeed life is but a dream—especially for those of us who have never kept a diary or possessed a note-book in their lives.

1

In this extremity I had recourse to another friend of Stephen Crane, who had appreciated him intuitively almost as soon as I did myself and who is a woman of excellent memory. My wife's recollection is that Crane and I met in London in October, 1897, and that he came to see us for the first time in our Essex home in the following November.

I have mentioned in a short paper written two years ago that it was Mr. S. S. Pawling, partner in the publishing firm of Mr. Heinemann, who brought us together. It was done at Stephen Crane's own desire.

I was told by Mr. Pawling that when asked whom he wanted to meet Crane mentioned two names, of which one was of a notable journalist (who had written some novels) whom he knew in America, I believe, and the other was mine. At that time the only facts we knew about each other were that we both had the same publisher in England. The only other fact I knew about Stephen Crane was that he was quite a young man. I had of course read his "Red Badge of Courage" of which people were writing and talking at that time. I certainly did not know that he had the slightest notion of my existence, or that he had seen a single line (there were not many of them then) of my writing. I can safely say that I earned this precious friendship by something like ten months of strenuous work with my pen. It took me just that time to write "The

Nigger of the Narcissus" working at what I always considered a very high pressure. It was on the ground of the authorship of that book that Crane wanted to meet me. Nothing could have been more flattering, than to discover that the author of "The Red Badge of Courage" appreciated my effort to present a group of men held together by a common loyalty and a common perplexity in a struggle not with human enemies but with the hostile conditions testing their faithfulness to the conditions of their own calling.

Apart from the imaginative analysis of his own temperament tried by the emotions of a battle-field Stephen Crane dealt in his book with the psychology of the mass—the army; while I—in mine —had been dealing with the same subject on a much smaller scale and in more specialized conditions—the crew of a merchant ship, brought to the test of what I may venture to call the moral problem of conduct. This may be thought a very remote connection between these two works and the idea may seem too far-fetched to be mentioned here; but that was my undoubted feeling at the time. It is a fact that I considered Crane, by virtue of his creative experience with "The Red Badge of Courage," as eminently fit to pronounce a judgment on my first consciously planned attempt to render the truth of a phase of life in the terms of my own temperament with all the sincerity of which I was capable.

I had, of course, my own opinion as to what I had done; but I doubted whether anything of my ambitiously comprehensive aim would be understood. I was wrong there; but my doubt was excusable since I myself would have been hard put to it if requested to give my complex intentions the form of a concise and definite statement. In that period of misgivings which so often follows an accomplished task I would often ask myself who in the world could be interested in such a thing? It was after reading "The Red Badge" which came into my hands directly after its publication in England that I said to myself: "Here's a man who may understand—if he ever sees the book; though of course that would not mean that he would like it." I do not mean to say that I looked towards the author of "The Red Badge" as the only man in the world. It would have been stupid and ungrateful. I had the moral support of one or two intimate friends and the solid fact of Mr. W. H. Henley's acceptance of my tale for serial publication in "The New Review" to give me confidence, while I awaited the larger verdict.

It seems to me that in trying to recall my memories of Stephen Crane I have been talking so far only about myself; but that is unavoidable, since this introduction, which I am privileged to write, can only trace what is left on earth of our personal intercourse which was even more short and fleeting than it may appear from the record of dates.

October, 1897—May, 1900. And out of that beg-
garly tale of months must be deducted the time of
his absence from England during the Spanish-American war, and of his visit to the United States shortly
before the beginning of his last illness. Even when he
was in England our intercourse was not so close and
frequent as the warmth of our friendship would have
wished it to be. We both lived in the country and,
though not very far from each other, in different
counties. I had my work to do, always in conditions
which made it a matter of urgency. He had his own
tasks and his own visions to attend to. I do not
think that he had more friendships to claim him
than I, but he certainly had more acquaintances and
more calls on his time.

This was only natural. It must be remembered
that as an author he was my senior, as I used to
remind him now and then with affected humility
which always provoked his smiles. He had a quiet
smile that charmed and frightened one. It made
you pause by something revelatory it cast over his
whole physiognomy, not like a ray but like a shadow.
I often asked myself what it could be, that quality
that checked one's care-free mood and now I think I
have had my answer. It was the smile of a man who
knows that his time will not be long on this earth.

I would not for a moment wish to convey the
impression of melancholy in connection with my
memories of Stephen Crane. I saw his smile first

over the table-cloth in a restaurant. We shook
hands with intense gravity and a direct stare at each
other, after the manner of two children told to make
friends. It was under the encouraging gaze of Sidney
Pawling who, a much bigger man than either of us
and possessed of a deep voice, looked like a grown-up
person entertaining two strange small boys—protect-
ing and slightly anxious as to the experiment. He
knew very little of either of us. I was a new author
and Crane was a new arrival. It was the meeting
of "The Red Badge" and "The Nigger" in the
presence of their publisher; but as far as our person-
alities went we were three strangers breaking bread
together for the first time. Yet it was as pleasantly
easy a meal as any I can remember. Crane talked
in his characteristic deliberate manner about Greece,
at war. I had already sensed the man's intense
earnestness underlying his quiet surface. Every
time he raised his eyes that secret quality (for his
voice was careless) of his soul was betrayed in a
clear flash. Most of the true Stephen Crane was in
his eyes, most of his strength at any rate, though it
was apparent also in his other features, as for
instance in the structure of his forehead, the deep
solid arches under the fair eyebrows.

Some people saw traces of weakness in the lower
part of his face. What I could see there was a hint of
the delicacy of sentiment, of the inborn fineness of nature which this man, whose life had been anything

but a stroll through a rose-garden, had managed to preserve like a sacred heritage. I say heritage, not acquisition, for it was not and could not have been acquired. One could depend on it on all occasions; whereas the cultivated kind is apt to show ugly gaps under very slight provocation. The coarseness of the professedly delicate must be very amusing to the misanthrope. But Crane was no enemy of his kind. That sort of thing did not amuse him. As to his own temper it was proof against anger and scorn, as I can testify, having seen him both angry and scornful, always quietly, on fitting occasions. Contempt and indignation never broke the surface of his moderation simply because he had no surface. He was all through of the same material, incapable of affectation of any kind, of any pitiful failure of generosity for the sake of personal advantage, or even from sheer exasperation which must find its relief.

Many people imagined him a fiery individuality. Certainly he was not cold-blooded. But his was an equable glow, morally and temperamentally. I would have said the same of his creative power (I have seen him sit down before a blank sheet of paper, dip his pen, write the first line at once and go on without haste and without pause for a couple of hours), had he not confided to me that his mentality did flag at times. I do not think it was anything more than every writer is familiar with at times. Another man would have talked of his "failing inspiration." It is very characteristic of Crane that I have never heard him use that word when talking about his work.

His phraseology was generally of a very modest cast. That unique and exquisite faculty, which Edward Garnet, another of his friends, found in his writing—"of disclosing an individual scene by an odd simile" was not apparent in his conversation. It was interesting of course, but its charm consisted mainly in the freshness of his impressions set off by an acute simplicity of view and expressed with an amusing deliberation. Super-abundance of words was not his failing when communing with those whom he liked and felt he could trust. With the other kind of "friends" he followed the method of a sort of suspended silence. On a certain occasion (it was at Brede Place) after two amazingly conceited idiots had gone away I said to him, "Stevie, you brood like a distant thunder-cloud." He had retired early to the other end of the room, and from there had sent out, now and then, a few words, more like the heavy drops of rain that precede the storm than growls of thunder. Poor Crane if he could look black enough at times, never thundered; though I have no doubt he could have been dangerous if he had liked. There always seemed to be something (not timidity) which restrained him, not from within but, I could not help fancying, from outside, with an effect as of a whis-

pered *memento mori* in the ear of a reveller not lost
to the sense of grace.

That of course was a later impression. It must
be stated clearly that I know very little of Stephen
Crane's life. We did not feel the need to tell each
other formally the story of our lives. That did not
prevent us from being very intimate and also very
open with each other from the first. Our affection
would have been "everlasting" as he himself quali-
fied it, had not the jealous death intervened with her
cruel capriciousness by striking down the younger
man. Our intimacy was really too close to admit of
indiscretions; not that he did not speak amusingly
of his experiences and of his hardships, and warmly
of the men that helped him in his early days, like
Mr. Hamlin Garland for instance, or men kindly
encouraging to him, like Mr. Howells. Many other
names he used to utter lovingly have been forgotten
by me after so many years.

It is a fact that I heard more of his adventures
than of his trials, privations and difficulties. I know
he had many. He was the least recriminatory of
men (though one of the most sensitive, I should
say), but, in any case, nothing I could have learned
would have shaken the independent judgment I
had formed for myself of his trustworthiness as a
man and a friend. Though the word is discredited
now and may sound pretentious, I will say that there

was in Crane a strain of chivalry which made him safe to trust with one's life. To be recognizably a man of honour carries no immunity against human weaknesses, but comports more rigid limitations in personal relations than the status of an "honourable man," however recognizable that too may be. Some men are "honourable" by courtesy, others by the office they hold, or simply by belonging to some popular assembly, the election to which is not generally secured by a dignified accuracy of statement and a scrupulous regard for the feelings of others. Many remain honourable (because of their great circumspection in the conduct of their affairs) without holding within themselves any of these restraints which are inherent in the character of a man of honour, however weak or luckless he may be.

I do not know everything about the strength of Crane's circumspection, but I am not afraid of what the biography which follows may disclose to us; though I am convinced that it will be free from hypocritical reservations. I think I have understood Stephen Crane, and from my too short acquaintance with his biographer I am confident he will receive the most humane and sympathetic treatment. What I discovered very early in our acquaintance was that Crane had not the face of a lucky man. That certitude came to me at our first meeting while I sat opposite him listening to his simple tales of Greece, while M. S.

Pawling presided at the initiatory feast—friendly and debonair, looking solidly anchored in the stream of life, and very reassuring, like a big, prosperous ship to the sides of which we two in our tossing little barks could hook on for safety. He was interested in the tales too; and the best proof of it is that when he looked at his watch and jumped up, saying, "I must leave you two now," it was very near four o'clock. Nearly a whole afternoon wasted, for an English business man.

No such consideration of waste or duty agitated Crane and myself. The sympathy that, even in regard of the very few years allotted to our friendship, may be said to have sprung up instantaneously between us, was the most undemonstrative case of that sort in the last century. We not only did not tell each other of it (which would have been missish) but even without entering formally into a previous agreement to remain together we went out and began to walk side by side in the manner of two tramps without home, occupation, or care for the next night's shelter. We certainly paid no heed to direction. The first thing I noticed were the Green Park railings, when to my remark that he had seen no war before he went to Greece Crane made answer: "No. But the 'Red Badge' is all right." I assured him that I never had doubted it; and, since the title of the work had been pronounced for the first time, feeling I must do something to show I

had read it, I said shyly: "I like your General."
He knew at once what I was alluding to but said
not a word. Nothing could have been more tramp-
like than our silent pacing, elbow to elbow, till,
after we had left Hyde Park Corner behind us,
Crane uttered with his quiet earnestness, the
words: "I like your young man—I can just see
him." Nothing could have been more characteristic
of the depth of our three-hour old intimacy than
that each of us should have selected for praise the
merest by-the-way vignette of a minor character.

This was positively the only allusion we made that
afternoon to our immortal works. Indeed we talked
very little of them at any time, and then always se-
lecting some minor point for particular mention;
which, after all, is not a bad way of showing an affectionate appreciation of a piece of work done by a
friend. A stranger would have expected more, but, in
a manner of speaking, Crane and I had never been
strangers. We took each other's work for granted
from the very first, I mean from the moment we
had exchanged those laudatory remarks alongside
the Green Park railings. Henceforth mutual recognition kept to that standard. It consisted often of
an approving grunt, sometimes of the mention of
some picked out paragraph, or of a line or only of a
few words that had caught our fancy and would, for
a time, be applied more or less aptly to the turns of
our careless, or even serious, talks.

Thus, for instance, there was a time when I persecuted poor Crane with the words "barbarously abrupt." They occur in that marvellous story "The Open Boat" and are applied by him to the waves of the sea (as seen by men tossing in a small dinghy) with an inspired audacity of epithet which was one of Crane's gifts that gave me most delight. How amazingly apt these words are where they stand, anybody can see by looking at that story, which is altogether a big thing, and has remained an object of my confirmed admiration. I was always telling Crane that this or that was "barbarously abrupt," or begging him not to be so "barbarously abrupt" himself, with a keen enjoyment of the incongruity; for no human being could be less abrupt than Crane. As to his humanity (in contra-distinction to barbarity) it was a shining thing without a flaw. It is possible that he may have grown at length weary of my little joke but he invariably received it with a smile, thus proving his consistent humanity toward his kind. But, after all, he too liked that story of his, of four men in a very small boat, which by the deep and simple humanity of presentation seems somehow to illustrate the essentials of life itself, like a symbolic tale. It opens with a phrase that anybody could have uttered but which, in relation to what is to follow, acquires the poignancy of a meaning almost universal. Once, much later in our acquaintance, I made use of it to him. He

came on a flying visit to Pent Farm where we were
living then. I noticed that he looked harassed. I,
too, was feeling for the moment as if things were
getting too much for me. He lay on the couch and
I sat on a chair opposite. After a longish silence
in which we both could have felt how uncertain
was the issue of life envisaged as a deadly adventure in which we were both engaged like two men
trying to keep afloat in a small boat, I said suddenly
across the width of the mantel-piece.

"None of them knew the colour of the sky."

He raised himself sharply. The words had struck
him as familiar, though I believe he failed to place
them at first. "Don't you know that quotation?" I
asked. (These words form the opening sentence of
his tale.) The startled expression passed off his face.
"Oh, yes," he said quietly, and lay down again.
Truth to say it was a time when neither he nor I had
the leisure to look up idly at the sky. The waves
just then were too "barbarously abrupt."

I do not mean to say that it was always so. Now
and then we were permitted to snatch a glance at
the colour of the sky. But it is a fact that in the
history of our essentially undemonstrative friendship (which is nearly as difficult to recapture as a
dream) that first long afternoon is the most care-free
instant, and the only one that had a character of
enchantment about it. It was spread out over a
large portion of central London. After the Green

Park the next thing I remember are the Kensington Gardens where under the lofty and historical trees I was vouchsafed a glimpse of the low mesquit bush overspreading the plum-coloured infinities of the great Texas plains. Then after a long tramp amongst an orderly multitude of grimy brick houses—from which the only things I carried off were the impressions of the coloured rocks of Mexico (or was it Arizona?), and my first knowledge of a locality called the Painted Desert—there came suddenly Oxford Street. I don't know whether the inhabitants of London were keeping indoors or had gone into the country that afternoon, but I don't remember seeing any people in the streets except for a figure, now and then, unreal, flitting by, obviously negligible. The wheeled traffic, too, was stopped; yet, it seems, not entirely, because I remember Crane seizing my arm and jerking me back on the pavement with the calm remark: "You will get run over." I love to think that the dear fellow had saved my life and that it seemed to amuse him. As to London's enormous volume of business all I know is that one A. B. C. shop had remained open. We went through the depressing ceremony of having tea there; but our interest in each other mitigated its inherent horrors and gave me a good idea of Crane's stoicism. At least I suppose we had tea, otherwise they would not have let us sit there so long. To be left alone was all we wanted. Neither of us had then a club to entertain the other in.   It will give a good notion of our indomitable optimism (on that afternoon) when I say that it was there, in those dismal surroundings, we reached the conclusion that though the world had grown old and weary, yet the scheme of creation remained as obscure as ever, and (from our own particular point of view) there was still much that was interesting to expect from Gods and men.

As if intoxicated by this draught of hope we rolled out of that A. B. C. shop, but I kept my head sufficiently to guess what was coming and to send a warning telegram to my wife in our Essex home.   Crane then was, I believe, staying temporarily in London.   But he seemed to have no care in the world; and so we resumed our tramping— east and north and south again, steering through uncharted mazes the streets, forgetting to think of dinner but taking a rest here and there, till we found ourselves, standing in the middle of Piccadilly Circus, blinking at the lights like two authentic night-birds. By that time we had been (in Tottenham Court Road) joined by Balzac.   How he came in I have no idea.   Crane was not given to literary curiosities of that kind.   Somebody he knew, or something he had read, must have attracted lately his attention to Balzac.   And now suddenly at ten o'clock in the evening he demanded insistently to be told in particular detail all about the Comédie Humaine, its

contents, its scope, its plan, and its general signifi-
cance, together with a critical description of Balzac's
style. I told him hastily that it was just black on
white; and for the rest, I said, he would have to wait
till we got across to Monico and had eaten some
supper. I hoped he would forget Balzac and his
Comédie. But not a bit of it; and I had no option
but to hold forth over the remnants of a meal, in
the rush of hundreds of waiters and the clatter of
tons of crockery, caring not what I said (for what
could Stephen want with Balzac), in the comfortable
assurance that the Monstrous Shade, even if led by
some strange caprice to haunt the long room of
Monico's, did not know enough English to understand a single word I said. I wonder what Crane
made of it all. He did not look bored, and
it was eleven o'clock before we parted at the foot
of that monumentally heavy abode of frivolity, the
Pavilion, with just a hand-shake and a good-night—
no more—without making any arrangements for
meeting again, as though we had lived in the same
town from childhood and were sure to run across
each other next day.

It struck me directly I left him that we had not
even exchanged addresses; but I was not uneasy.
Sure enough, before the month was out there arrived
a post card (from Ravensbrook) asking whether he
might come to see us. He came, was received as an
old friend, and before the end of the day conquered

my wife's sympathy, as undemonstrative and sincere as his own quiet friendliness. The friendship that sprang up between them was confirmed by the interest Crane displayed in our first child, a boy who came on the scene not quite two months afterwards. How strong was that interest on the part of Stephen Crane and his wife in the boy is evidenced by the fact that at the age of six weeks he was invited to come for a long visit to Ravensbrook. He was in fact impatiently expected there. He arrived in state bringing with him not only his parents but also a young aunt, and was welcomed like a prince. This visit, during which I suffered from a sense of temporary extinction, is commemorated by a group photograph taken by an artist summoned with his engine (regardless of expense) to Ravensbrook. Though the likenesses are not bad it is a very awful thing. Nobody looks like him or herself in it. The best yet are the Crane dogs, a very important part of the establishment and quite conscious of it, belonging apparently to some order of outlandish poodles, amazingly sedate and yet the most restless animals I have ever met. They pervaded, populated and filled the whole house. Whichever way one looked at any time, down the passage, up the stairs, into the drawing-room, there was always a dog in sight. Had I been asked on the first day how many there were I would have guessed about thirty. As a matter of fact there were only three, but I think they never sat down, except in Crane's study, where they had their entrée at all hours.

A scratching would be heard at the door, Crane would drop his pen with alacrity to throw it open— and the dogs would enter sedately in single file, taking a lot of time about it, too. Then the room would resound for a while with grunts, sniffs, yawns, heavy flops, followed by as much perhaps as three whole minutes of silence. Then the dogs would get up, one after another, never all together, and direct their footsteps to the door in an impressive and ominous manner. The first arrival waited considerably for the others before trying to attract attention by means of scratching on the bottom panel. Then, never before, Crane would raise his head, go meekly to the door— and the procession would file out at the slowest possible pace. The recurrent sedateness of the proceedings, the utter unconsciousness of the dogs, dear Stephen's absurd gravity while playing his part in those ceremonies, without ever a muscle of his face moving, were irresistibly, exasperatingly funny. I tried to preserve my gravity (or at least to keep calm), with fair success. Only one afternoon on the fifth or sixth repetition I could not help bursting into a loud interminable laugh and then the dear fellow asked me in all innocence what was the matter. I managed to conceal my nervous irritation from him and he never learned the secret of that laugh in which there was a beginning of hysteria.

If the definition that man is a laughing animal be true then Crane was neither one nor the other; indeed he was but a hurried visitor on this earth on which he had so little reason to be joyous.   I might say that I never heard him laugh, except in connection with the baby.   He loved children; but his friendship with our child was of the kind that put our mutual sentiment, by comparison, somewhere within the arctic region.   The two could not be compared; at least I have never detected Crane stretched full length and sustained on his elbows on a grass plot, in order to gaze at me; on the other hand this was his usual attitude of communion with the small child —with him who was called *the Boy,* and whose destiny it was to see more war before he came of age than the author of "The Red Badge" had time to see in all the allotted days of his life.   In the gravity of its disposition the baby came quite up to Crane; yet those two would sometimes find something to laugh at in each other.   Then there would be silence, and glancing out of the low window of my room I would see them, very still, staring at each other with a solemn understanding that needed no words or perhaps was beyond words altogether.   I could not object on any ground to their profound intimacy but I do not see why Crane should have developed such an unreasonable suspicion as to my paternal efficiency.   He seemed to be everlastingly taking the boy's part.   I could not see that the baby was being oppressed, hectored over, or in any way deprived of its rights, or ever wounded in its feelings by me; but Crane seemed always to nurse some vague unexpressed grievance as to my conduct. I was inconsiderate. For instance—why could I not get a dog for the boy? One day he made me quite a scene about it. He seemed to imply I should drop everything and go look for a dog. I sat under the storm and said nothing. At last he cried "Hang it all, a boy ought to have a dog." It was an appeal to first principles but for an answer I pointed at the window and said: "Behold the boy." . . . He was sitting on a rug spread on the grass, with his little red stocking-cap very much over one eye (a fact of which he seemed unaware), and propped round with many pillows on account of his propensity to roll over on his side helplessly. My answer was irresistible. This is one of the few occasions on which I heard Stephen Crane laugh outright. He dropped his preaching on the dog theme and went out to the boy while I went on with my work. But he was strangely incorrigible. When he came back after an hour or so, his first words were, "Joseph, I will teach your boy to ride." I closed with the offer at once—but it was not to be. He was not given the time.

The happiest mental picture my wife and I preserve of Crane is on the occasion of our first visit to Brede Place when he rode to meet us at the Park gate. He looked at his best on horseback. On that day he must have been feeling well. As usual, he was happy in the saddle. As he went on trotting by the side of the open trap I said to him: "If you give the boy your seat I will be perfectly satisfied." I knew this would please him; and indeed his face remained wreathed in smiles all the way to the front door. He looked about him at that bit of the world, down the green slopes and up the brown fields, with an appreciative serenity and the confident bearing of a man who is feeling very sure of the present and of the future. All because he was looking at life from the saddle, with a good morning's work behind him. Nothing more is needed to give a man a blessed moment of illusion. The more I think of that morning the more I believe it was just that; that it had really been given me to see Crane perfectly happy for a couple of hours; and that it was under this spell that directly we arrived he led me impatiently to the room in which he worked when at Brede. After we got there he said to me, "Joseph, I will give you something." I had no idea what it would be, till I saw him sit down to write an inscription in a very slim volume. He presented it to me with averted head. It was "The Black Riders." He had never spoken to me of his verse before. It was while holding the book in my hand that I learned that they were written years before in America. I expressed my appreciation of them that afternoon in the usual half a dozen, or dozen, words which we allowed ourselves when completely pleased with each other's work. When the pleasure was not so complete the words would be many. And that was a great waste of breath and time. I must confess that we were no critics, I mean temperamentally. Crane was even less of a critic than myself. Criticism is very much a matter of a vocabulary, very consciously used; with us it was the intonation that mattered. The tone of a grunt could convey an infinity of meaning between us.

The articulate literary conscience at our elbow was Edward Garnett. He, of course, was worth listening to. His analytical appreciation (or appreciative analysis) of Crane's art, in the London Academy of 17th Dec., 1898,[1] goes to the root of the matter with Edward's almost uncanny insight, and a well balanced sympathy with the blind, pathetic striving of the artist towards a complete realization of his individual gift. How highly Edward Garnett rated Crane's gift is recorded in the conclusions of that admirable and, within the limits of its space, masterly article of some two columns, where at the end are set down such affirmative phrases as: "The chief impressionist of the age." . . . "Mr. Crane's talent is unique" . . . and where he hails him as

[1] Extended and re-published in the volume "Friday Nights." Alfred A. Knopf. 1922. New York.

"the creator of fresh rhythms and phrases," while the very last words state confidently that: "Undoubtedly, of the young school it is Mr. Crane who is the genius—the others have their talents."

My part here being not that of critic but of private friend all I will say is that I agreed warmly at the time with that article which from the quoted phrases might be supposed a merely enthusiastic pronouncement, but on reading will be found to be based on that calm sagacity which Edward Garnett, for all his fiery zeal in the cause of letters, could always summon for the judgment of matters emotional—as all response to the various forms of art must be in the main. I had occasion to re-read it last year in its expanded form in a collection of literary essays of great, now almost historical, interest in the record of American and English imaginative literature. I found there a passage or two, not bearing precisely on Crane's work but giving a view of his temperament, on which of course his art was based; and of the conditions moral and material under which he had to put forth his creative faculties and his power of steady composition. On those matters, as a man who had the opportunity to look at Crane's life in England I wish to offer a few remarks before closing my contribution to the memory of my friend.

I do not know that he was ever dunned for money

and had to work under a threat of legal proceedings.
I don't think he was ever dunned in the sense in which
such a phrase is used about a spendthrift unscrupu-
lous in incurring debts. No doubt he was sometimes
pressed for money. He lived by his pen and the
prices he obtained were not great. Personally he was
not extravagant; and I will not quarrel with him
for not choosing to live in a garret. The tenancy
of Brede Place was held by him-at a nominal rent.
That glorious old place was not restored then, and
the greatest part of it was uninhabitable. The
Cranes had furnished in a modest way six or seven
of the least dilapidated rooms, which even then
looked bare and half empty. Certainly there was
a horse, and at one time even two, but that luxury
was not so very expensive at that time. One man
looked after them. Riding was the only exercise
open to Crane; and if he did work so hard surely
he was entitled to some relaxation, if only for the
preservation of his unique talent.

His greatest extravagance was hospitality of which
I, too, had my share; often in the company, I am
sorry to say, of men who after sitting at his board
chose to speak of him and of his wife slightingly.
Having some rudimentary sense of decency their behaviour while actually under the Cranes' roof often
produced on me a disagreeable impression. Once I
ventured to say to him, "You are too good-natured,
Stephen." He gave me one of his quiet smiles, that

seemed to hint so poignantly at the vanity of all things, and after a period of silence remarked: "I am glad those Indians are gone." He was surrounded by men who secretly envious, hostile to the real quality of his genius (and a little afraid of it), were also in antagonism with the essential fineness of his nature. But enough of them. *Pulvis et umbra sunt.* I mean even those that may be alive yet. They were ever hardly anything else; one would have forgotten them if it were not for the legend (if one may dignify perfidious and contemptible gossip by that name), they created in order to satisfy that same obscure instinct of base humanity, which in the past would often bring against any exceptional man the charge of consorting with the devil. It was just as vague, just as senseless and in its implications just as lying as the mediaeval kind. I have heard one of these "friends" hint before several other Philistines that Crane could not write his tales without getting drunk!

Putting aside the gross palpable stupidity of such a statement—which the creature gave out as an instance of the artistic temperament—I am in a position to disclose what may have been the foundation of this piece of gossip. I have seen repeatedly Crane at work. A small jug of still smaller ale would be brought into the study at about ten o'clock; Crane would pour out some of it into a glass and settle himself at the long table at which he used to write in Brede Place. I would take a book and settle myself at the other end of the same table, with my back to him; and for two hours or so not a sound would be heard in that room. At the end of that time Crane would say suddenly: "I won't do any more now, Joseph." He would have covered three of his large sheets with his regular, legible, perfectly controlled, handwriting, with no more than half a dozen erasures—mostly single words—in the whole lot. It seemed to me always a perfect miracle in the way of mastery over material and expression. Most of the ale would be still in the glass, and how flat by that time I don't like to think! The most amusing part was to see Crane, as if moved by some obscure sense of duty, drain the last drop of that untempting remnant before we left the room to stroll to and fro in front of the house while waiting for lunch. Such is the origin of some of these gleeful whispers making up the Crane legend of "unrestrained temperament." I have known various sorts of temperaments—some perfidious and some lying—but "unrestrained temperament" is mere parrot talk. It has no meaning. But it was suggestive. It was founded on Crane's visits to town during which I more than once met him there. We used to spend afternoons and evenings together and I did not see any of his supposed revels in progress; nor yet have I ever detected any after effects of them on any occasion. Neither have

I ever seen anybody who would own to having been
a partner in those excesses—if only to the extent
of standing by charitably—which would have been
a noble part to play.   I daresay all those "excesses"
amounted to very little more than the one in which
he asked me to join him in the following letter.   It
is the only note I have kept from the very few which
we exchanged.   The reader will see why it is one
of my most carefully preserved possessions.

RAVENSBROOK.

OXTED.

17 March.   (1899)

"MY DEAR CONRAD: I am enclosing you a bit of
MS. under the supposition that you might like to
keep it in remembrance of my warm and endless
friendship for you.   I am still hoping that you will
consent to Stokes' invitation to come to the Savage
on Saturday night.   Cannot you endure it?   Give
my affectionate remembrances to Mrs. Conrad and
my love to the boy.

Yours always,

STEPHEN CRANE.

P.S.   You must accept says Cora—and I—our
invitation to come home with me on Sat. night.

I joined him.   We had a very amusing time with
the Savages.   Afterwards Crane refused to go home
till the last train.   Evidence of what somebody has

called his "unrestrained temperament," no doubt.
So we went and sat at Gatti's, I believe; unless it
was in a Bodega which existed then in that neighbourhood, and talked. I have a vivid memory of
this awful debauch because it was on that evening
that Crane told me of a subject for a story—a very
exceptional thing for him to do. He called it "The
Predecessor." I could not recall now by what ca-
pricious turns and odd associations of thought he
reached the enthusiastic conclusion that it would
make a good play, and that we must do it together.
He wanted me to share in a certain success—"a
dead sure thing," he said. His was an unrestrain-
edly generous temperament. But let that pass. I
must have been specially predisposed, because I
caught the infection at once. There and then we began to build up the masterpiece, interrupting each
other eagerly, for, I don't know how it was, the air
around us had suddenly grown thick with felicitous
suggestions. We carried on this collaboration as
far as the railway time-table would let us, and then
made a break for the last train. Afterwards we
did talk of our collaboration now and then, but no
attempt at it was ever made. Crane had other
stories to write; I was immersed deeply in "Lord
Jim," of which I had to keep up the instalments in
"Blackwood"; difficulties in presenting the subject on
the stage rose one after another before our experience. The general subject consisted in a man

personating his "predecessor" (who had died) in the
hope of winning a girl's heart. The scenes were to
include a ranch at the foot of the Rocky Mountains,
I remember, and the action I fear would have been
frankly melodramatic. Crane insisted that one of
the situations should present the man and the girl
on a boundless plain standing by their dead ponies
after a furious ride (a truly Crane touch). I made
some objections. A boundless plain in the light of
a sunset could be got into a back-cloth, I admitted;
but I doubted whether we could induce the management of any London theatre to deposit two stuffed
horses on its stage.

Recalling now those earnestly fantastic discussions it occurs to me that Crane and I must
have been unconsciously penetrated by a prophetic
sense of the technique and of the very spirit
of film-plays of which even the name was unknown then to the world. But if gifted with prophetic sense we must have been strangely ignorant
of ourselves, since it must be obvious to any one
who has read a page of our writings that a collaboration between us two could never come to anything in the end—could never even have been begun. The project was merely the expression of our
affection for each other. We were fascinated for a
moment by the will-of-the-wisp of close artistic communion. It would in no case have led us into a
bog. I flatter myself we both had too much re-

gard for each other's gifts not to be clear-eyed about them. We would not have followed the lure very far. At the same time it can not be denied that there were profound, if not extensive, similitudes in our temperaments which could create for a moment that fascinating illusion. It is not to be regretted, for it had, at any rate, given us some of the most light-hearted moments in the clear but sober atmosphere of our intimacy. From the force of circumstances there could not be much sunshine in it. "None of them saw the colour of the sky!" And alas! it stood already written that it was the younger man who would fail to make a landing through the surf. So I am glad to have that episode to remember, a brotherly serio-comic interlude, played under the shadow of coming events. But I would not have alluded to it at all if it had not come out in the course of my most interesting talk with the author of this biography, that Crane had thought it worth while to mention it in his correspondence, whether seriously or humorously, I know not. So here it is without the charm which it had for me but which can not be reproduced in the mere relation of its outward characteristics: a clear gleam on us two, succeeded by the Spanish-American war into which Crane disappeared like a wilful man walking away into the depths of an ominous twilight.

The cloudy afternoon when we two went rushing

all over London together, was for him the beginning of the end. The problem was to find £60
that day, before the sun set, before dinner, before the "six forty" train to Oxted, at once, that
instant—lest peace should be declared and the opportunity of seeing a war be missed. I had not
£60 to lend him. Sixty shillings was nearer my
mark. We tried various offices but had no luck,
or rather we had the usual luck of money hunting
enterprises. The man was either gone out to see
about a dog, or would take no interest in the Spanish-
American war. In one place the man wanted to
know what was the hurry? He would have liked to
have forty-eight hours to think the matter over.
As we came downstairs Crane's white-faced excitement frightened me. Finally it occurred to me to
take him to Messrs. William Blackwood & Sons'
London office. There he was received in a most
friendly way. Presently I escorted him to Charing
Cross where he took the train for home with the
assurance that he would have the means to start
"for the war" next day. That is the reason I can
not to this day read his tale "The Price of the Harness" without a pang. It has done nothing more
deadly than pay his debt to Messrs. Blackwood;
yet now and then I feel as though that afternoon
I had led him by the hand to his doom. But,
indeed, I was only the blind agent of the fate
that had him in her grip! Nothing could have

held him back. He was ready to swim the ocean.

Thirteen years afterwards I made use, half consciously, of the shadow of the primary idea of the
"Predecessor," in one of my short tales which were
serialized in the *Metropolitan Magazine*. But in
that tale the dead man in the background is not a
Predecessor but merely an assistant on a lonely
plantation; and instead of the ranch, the mountains and the plains, there is a cloud-capped island,
a bird-haunted reef and the sea. All this the mere
distorted shadow of what we two used to talk about
in a fantastic mood; but now and then, as I wrote,
I had the feeling that he had the right to come and
look over my shoulder. But he never came. I
received no suggestions from him, subtly conveyed
without words. There will never be any collaboration for us now. But I wonder, were he alive
whether he would be pleased with the tale. I don't
know. Perhaps not. Or, perhaps, after picking up
the volume with that detached air I remember so
well, and turning over page after page in silence,
he would suddenly read aloud a line or two and
then looking straight into my eyes as was his wont
on such occasions, say with all the intense earnestness of affection that was in him: "I—like—that,
Joseph."

JOSEPH CONRAD.

I

SUNNY BLUE

THE birth of his fourteenth child so distracted Jonathan Townley Crane, D.D., that a letter went unfinished until the next day, when he neatly changed its date from November 1 to November 2, 1871 and concluded: "I was interrupted yesterday and did not send this to the Post Office. Mrs. Crane sends her regards. The new baby is a boy and we have named him Stephen for his ancestor who signed the Declaration."

This naming of the new baby must have been important in the gentle, elderly man's mind. Master Edmund Crane, aged thirteen, took the letter to the post and tumbled on the steep front steps of 14 Mulberry Place, Newark, New Jersey, dreadfully bruising his knee. So Jonathan Crane wrote, a week later: "Mrs. Crane is still alarmed for Ed's knee which continues painful but the baby is very good and quiet. We have named him Stephen because it is an old name in the Crane family." And the family was old in the State of New Jersey, largely lettered on grants of land and the documents of two wars; there were

Cranes in the colony when Anne was queen of England; the Crane who figured in the Continental Congress had his coat armor painted on the flaps of his saddle bag. Plainly, the good and quiet baby was named with care.

He was good and quiet and frail. In the spring of 1872 Jonathan Crane halted a sermon in the Central Methodist Church with a blunt statement that Stephen was ill and needed him. There were eight older children living but Stephen had arrived in this surprising and belated fashion. Sermons and the writing of controversial pamphlets were suspended when Stephen took cold. He took cold with regularity and his first appearances in the solid society of Mulberry Place were made as an attachment to a monstrous red silk handkerchief which he liked immensely as a plaything and dropped into the aisle of his father's church, cutting the drift of a sermon with wails until somebody brought it back and his parent could go on talking slowly of the necessity of foreign missions and the danger of frivolous amusements to the youth of his sect.

Jonathan Crane came of Presbyterian stock but it appears that, as an undergraduate of Princeton, he was disturbed about a point in Presbyterian dogma: did the souls of unbaptized infants go to hell? It seemed hardly just. Methodism offered an escape from the problem and gave his controversial abilities fuller scope. He delighted in argument but argu-

ment must be kept within the bounds of breeding.
Once some cruder Christian flung at him in debate,
"Brother Crane never forgets that he is a gentleman!" and Jonathan Crane retorted, "Why should I,
sir?"

He wrote a good, severe prose and some of his
ideas remain interesting. He had, like Somerset
Maugham, deep doubts as to the intentions of mis-
sionaries. The Word must be spread but "by all
means the candidates for the post of missionary
should be strictly examined as to their motives in
undertaking these duties. We hear grave reports of
some who domineer and oppress these childish intellects committed to their care and it can not be
doubted that some of our brethren seek to exalt their
own station and that some are more interested to
clothe the naked bodies of the heathen than to en-
lighten their minds." And he had doubts about the
sanctity of small towns: "I am much more concerned that we should live truthfully and kindly here
than that we should be busy in condemning the luxuries and sins of New York City." And he had
doubts about the Christian Temperance Union
League when four ladies from Ohio came to consult
his wife on the subject in 1873: "Mrs. Crane is
much impressed by this project. I do not think it
exactly practical . . . but they mean very well. Little Stephen has a bad cold this week."

Stephen had become the pet of the family. Only

his mother could brush the fair, soft hair which curled a little and he was always shown to callers at the plain brick house.   In 1873 young Richard Watson Gilder brought a Miss Rutherford to see Mrs. Crane and Stephen fell in love with the girl.   He was discovered as an ornament of her red skirt when Mr. Gilder was squiring her around the corner of Market Street.   Enchanted by the conquest, she came back the next day with a toy for the baby but Stephen sat disdainfully in a corner and wouldn't look. Whenever Miss Rutherford wore red, though, he was hers completely.

The family taught him his letters and he showed a bright interest in the career of his biggest brother, Jonathan Townley Crane, Junior, cub reporter of the *Newark Advertiser*.   Mrs. Crane was the domestic dictionary and Townley would ask her how to spell adjectives of his articles.   The baby attended the process and becomes a personage with his first recorded question.   He was making symbols on a piece of paper in good imitation of the journalist and lifted up his voice to ask, "Ma, how do you spell 'O'?"

In 1874, Dr. Crane's time at the church in Newark was up; the family moved to Bloomington on the Raritan across from Bound Brook and Stephen was held on a white horse which he remembered twenty years later as a savage beast.   But it was no part of Mrs. Crane's theory that a child of hers should be

afraid of anything.   He was told to stay on the horse
and not to be scared.   Somebody threw a ball of
hard rubber too swiftly into his delicate hands with
thin bones; Mrs. Crane wiped his sapphire eyes and
told him that he mustn't cry.   She took him to the
religious frolics at Ocean Grove where he saw the
waves from the beach and had an atrocious dream of
black riders on black horses charging at him from
the long surf up the shore and so woke screaming,
night after night.   But, always, he must not cry.

His brothers took him to bathe in the Raritan
from a sandbar that jutted into the clear river near
the house, although both Miss Frances Willard
and Anthony Comstock had lately assured the world
that it was a disgusting and Unchristian thing for
any boy to be seen in an undressed condition outside
his own home.   However, he was taken to swim in
spite of the joint edict and his brothers were delighted
by his ambition.   He was left paddling in the shal-
lows but he wouldn't stay there.   He must get out
where Will or Ed was splashing and somebody would
fish him out just as his head disappeared.   Stevie
came up strangling but not afraid.   He missed the
river, it seems, when the Cranes spent a year in
Paterson and made a manful effort to climb down
into the Hudson from a pier of Jersey City when his
father was preaching there in 1877.   The straggling
port and a return to Paterson disagreed with him and
there is a legend that some doctor advised Jonathan

Crane to find duties in high air. So in 1879 the man of sixty left his native state and took charge of Methodism in Port Jervis, over the border.

Port Jervis was then a pretty town, splashed in white houses about the hills that were making northwestern New York known as a game preserve. Stephen improved and could be sent to school on his eighth birthday. He could read and write and was already learned in the moral adventures of Goody Twoshoes. The school at once annoyed him. Here he was debased and hemmed in by a pack of infants aged five and six. Humiliation dragged him forward and "they tell me that I got through two grades in six weeks which sounds like the lie of a fond mother at a teaparty but I do remember that I got ahead very fast and that father was pleased with me. He used to take me driving with him to little places near Port Jervis where he was going to preach or bury somebody. Once we got mixed up in an Irish funeral near a place named Slate Hill. Everybody was drunk and father was scandalized. . . . He was so simple and good that I often think he didn't know much of anything about humanity. Will, one of my brothers, gave me a toy gun and I tried to shoot a cow with it over at Middletown when father was preaching there and that upset him wonderfully. He liked all kinds of animals and never drove a horse faster than two yards an hour even if some Christian was dying somewhere. But it is a big job

to be presiding elder in a Methodist Conference.
He worked himself to death, my people thought."

Jonathan Crane had worked long and hard. He
had once been president of the Pennington Semi-
nary and was fond of boys who, he said, "should
be handled with great kindness and care as they
have often notions about justice in conduct far
beyond their years." So he was much distressed
when a lad named nothing less than Samuel Weller
wrote from Newark to say that he had been discharged from the shop of a good Methodist for
denying hell. The old man took his daughter
Agnes down to Newark and hunted other work for
Samuel Weller, caught cold on the way back to Port
Jervis and died suddenly, having preached the day
before.

He died and terror closed on his last child. People came from everywhere to lament Jonathan Crane.
Some country wife stood in the kitchen and sang
long hymns. Townley and George and Will and
Edmund were in black clothes; his mother sat in
the darkened parlour surrounded by whispering
women and, somehow, one of Stephen's hands
brushed the cold silver handle of the coffin; the full
horror of Christian death smashed on the lank child's
consciousness. "We tell kids that heaven is just
across the gaping grave and all that bosh and then
we scare them to glue with flowers and white sheets
and hymns. We ought to be crucified for it! . . .

I have forgotten nothing about this, not a damned iota, not a shred."

There followed penitential confusions. Mrs. Crane lived for some months in Roseville, outside Newark, and Stephen endured scarlet fever in a boarding house, but his mother had learned to like Port Jervis and Stephen had been well there. So he was brought back to the hills and played games patterned on "Black Dick of the Pony Express" and "The Terror of the Sagebrush" with other children. It was a good time—"a bully time"—afterwards. He could make up a game more quickly than the rest of the gang and brother Edmund gave him a quarter to get his long curls cropped, against Mrs. Crane's orders. She made for him mittens of the brightest red and he had red topped boots in winter when snow thickened on the paths after sumach's bloody flare had died from the hills. He was very well and happy. Wind whipped up colour in his pointed face and his mother let him go racing in the wake of grown men whose heels rang sharply on frozen earth, running past the house toward the wild glow of fires that reddened the whole night.

2

The tactful Matthew Arnold, on pilgrimage among us in 1883, told William Forester that Americans should get done with the Civil War as a topic; it

was a bore. The surgeon answered, "But so many
of us fought in it." The critic playfully retorted,
"That's no excuse. War is seldom fruitful or important." He then gave Dr. Forester a signed copy of
his note on the translation of Homer's Iliad, a
poem dealing with the siege of Troy and went somewhere else. As he recedes in the Victorian mist, it
sometimes seems that Matthew Arnold was singularly obtuse, for war happens to be a department of
æsthetic available, as is religion, to everybody.

The Civil War ceased physically in 1865 and its
political end may be reasonably expected about the
year 3000. As heroic legend its history has been
curious and remains unwritten because of that spirit-
ual censorship which strictly forbids the telling of
truth about any American record until the material
of such an essay is scattered and gone. How did
the men who scorched their youth and scarred their
bodies think of those four years, before the easy
sentiment of senility clouded down? One knows
that in 1868 General Custer's wife noted: "My
husband's troopers seem to have absolutely no un-
kind feeling toward the Secessionists at all and
they never talk about their triumphs and exploits.
They are always teasing each other about how badly
they fought and how many times they ran away.
It is distressing to see and hear how little exalted
their views are." And one knows that in 1869 at a
banquet of the Grand Army a man lifted his glass

and toasted, "Every one that ran at Shiloh, like I did!"

The distress of Mrs. Custer and the boredom of Matthew Arnold meet to supply a conjecture. The war did become a bore to foreigners and literary critics and the common man's attitude toward the myth of a pure, courageous host bent on the Lord's work was truly shocking. The swift cynicism of the American which is the basis of our popular thought rounded promptly on romantic views of the Rebellion. Duval, the leading ballad singer of New York was hissed from the stage in June of 1865 when he tried to please an audience speckled with soldiers by chanting, "Home Have Come Our Boys in Blue." The gunbearing animals shouted, "Dry up!" and "Sing something funny!" A pamphlet without signature was issued in Philadelphia before 1866 began and along with a wholly accurate account of the war's two last months, buyers were invited to believe that General Grant told masculine stories to his staff and that General Sheridan drank whisky before all men out of a silver flask. Both rumors have unofficially persisted to this day. There were songs current attributing mistresses to the popular Northern generals, doubtless due to an adolescent habit of making heroes in all things strenuous, and a New York publisher found that John Esten Cooke's frankly Southern novels, "Surry of Eagle's Nest" and "Mohun" sold most readily in the North although Cooke had not one flattering word to say of the Union forces and the Virginian himself wrote that "I am surprised by the number of handsome letters that come to hand from former soldiers of the enemy."

The war left almost nothing printed that the literate peasants and clerks who fought would recognize as the truth of their acts. In Cooke's "Mohun" one finds a rather vivid picture of collapsing Richmond with its intrigues, its profiteers and its frantic pleasures but the mind of the Virginian gentleman, trained on Lever and Dickens, shrank from the detail of the battlefield and his tales merely build a Pantheon for the South with central niches rightly reserved to the figures of Lee and Stonewall Jackson. He was honest and not too extravagant but he was no realist. There is no Northern fiction worth a glance and narrative reminiscences such as Warren Goss's "Recollections of a Private" were rare. Goss, the best of the narrators, was remorselessly pruned by his publisher even though his book succeeded among boys and soldiers on the ground of its frankness.

The realists sat on fences and the steps of stores in the sprawled depth of the nation and made a topic of the war when political campaigns and labour held no thrill. They might be flogged by acute orators into the ready ferocity of election days and Grand Army rallies but in 1870 James Russell Lowell found that stories of the battle line "obscene and horrible" were being told before young boys by the commonplace veterans of Cambridge, Massachusetts, and it is pretty evident that the realists on shady corners preferred war in form. A lad growing up in Ohio saw two men not yet middle aged come to blows about the rightful ownership of a pair of boots lost in the baking trenches before Vicksburg and a queerly sensitive child in upper New York may have heard and seen equal ironies. "An American," the sulphurous John Skidmore wrote in 1880, "has only three subjects—his work, the Rebellion and women. Owing to our freedom of speech he can only talk about the first subject in the company of ladies and Mr. Lowell is right in saying that our national conversation is dull as the ladies are most averse to hearing anything truthful about the war." The realists, one imagines, were restricted to the fence and the cornfield. But in 1883, a Miss Olive Brett came upon Stephen Crane digging her small nephew from the sands at Ocean Grove and was told that Johnny was a corpse foolishly planted by the burial squad while he still had a canteen full of whisky on him and that Stephen was his provident comrade retrieving supplies. This is not a child's fancy of battle; Stephen had been listening to some realist; Miss Brett was properly horrified and directly spanked him.

Now Stephen's brother William is remembered

by men who knew him as an undergraduate at Wesleyan as an expert in the strategy of Chancellorsville and Gettysburg. His brother Edmund yearly gave the boy volume after volume of Harry Castleman's "Frank" series. There were "Frank on a Gunboat" and "Frank on the Red River" and "Frank at Mobile Bay"—unpretentious and straightforward tales about a boy in the War written, apparently, for boys. There is no known biography of Harry Castleman but this oddity makes him interesting. Stephen adored these works. Mrs. Crane let him look at the monstrous flat tomes of the Harper's history of the Rebellion with their crude and romantic pictures and on rainy days, when the pictures palled, he poured all the buttons from his mother's store into battalions and regiments that marched and countermarched about his bony knees in an endless conflict, incomprehensible to the family. It was a private war.

There were other books, of course. When he was ten his sister Agnes gave him "Sir Wilfrid's Seven Flights," a thing printed for children by the moral Routledge but certainly the least moral book ever issued by his house with that aim, as the hero is a rake and all his adventures end in some frustrated scene. Sir Wilfrid sees El Dorado buried in its own golden sand and flings back the gift of eternal wisdom rather than live for ever with the revived Rhodope in her kingdom beneath the pyramids. Stephen liked it and a paragraph of the stiff, ornate prose Tom Hood claimed to have written came to the surface of his thought eighteen years later. "Sir Wilfrid's Seven Flights" must have affected him badly; in the summer of 1882 the kind Miss Brett tried to read him "A Christmas Carol" by Charles Dickens and Stephen went to sleep.

In 1883 Mrs. Crane moved to a small house in Asbury Park, New Jersey. Asbury Park was advertised widely in the nation as a resort quite free from sin but there was some mistake about that since Stephen was riding the retired circus pony his brother Townley had found for him along a road behind the seaside town in May of 1884 and he saw a white girl stabbed by her negro lover on the edge of a roadmaker's camp. He galloped the pony home and said nothing to Mrs. Crane although he was sweating with fright.

A strain of secrecy had developed in the slim boy or he knew that his mother's health was failing. Mary Crane had passed sixty, now, and no longer insisted that Stephen must be brave. She worried in the other extreme and told friends, "Stevie is like the wind in Scripture. He bloweth whither he listeth." He rode the pony into the ocean, to the admiration of other children, and clung to its bare back while it did tricks. He also pulled a somewhat older boy, Wallis McHarg, out of the surf and then told Wallis he would punch his jaw if the rescued

dared to tell Mrs. Crane they had been swimming
on Sunday.

"My mother was a very religious woman but I
don't think that she was as narrow as most of her
friends or her family—" She was Mary Helen Peck,
the child and sister of famous Methodist preachers;
"My brothers tell me that she got herself into trouble
before I was old enough to follow proceedings by
taking care of a girl who had an accidental baby.
Inopportune babies are not part of Methodist ritual
but mother was always more of a Christian than a
Methodist and she kept this girl at our house in
Asbury until she found a home somewhere.
Mother's friends were mostly women and they had
the famous feminine aversion to that kind of baby.
It is funny that women's interest in babies trickles
clean off the mat if they have never met papa so-
cially. . . . After my father died, mother lived
in and for religion. We had very little money.
Mother wrote articles for Methodist papers and reported for the (*New York*) *Tribune* and the (*Philadelphia*) *Press*. Every August she went down to
Ocean Grove and reported proceedings at the Methodist holy show there. . . . My brother Will used to
try to argue with her on religious subjects such as hell
but he always gave it up. Don't understand that
mother was bitter or mean but it hurt her that any
of us should be slipping from Grace and giving
up eternal damnation or salvation or those things.

You could argue just as well with a wave. . . . She was always starting off when she felt well enough to some big prayer meeting or experience meeting and she spoke very well. Her voice was something like Ellen Terry's but deeper. She spoke as slowly as a big clock ticks and her effects were impromptu. . . . It is in me to think that she did some good work for the public schools. One of my sisters was a teacher and mother tried for years to get women placed on the school boards and to see that whisky was not sold to boys under age. . . . I used to like church and prayer meetings when I was a kid but that cooled off and when I was thirteen or about that, my brother Will told me not to believe in Hell after my uncle had been boring me about the lake of fire and the rest of the sideshows. . . . Once when I was fourteen an organ grinder on the beach at Asbury gave me a nice long drink out of a nice red bottle for picking up his hat for him. I felt ecstatic walking home and then I was an Emperor and some Rajahs and Baron de Blowitz all at the same time. I had been sulky all morning and now I was perfectly willing to go to a prayer meeting and Mother was tickled to death. And, mind you, all because this nefarious Florentine gave me a red drink out of a bottle. I have frequently wondered how much mothers ever know about their sons, after all. She would not have found it much of a joke. . . ."

She was a woman of intense pride. She had been

educated more thoroughly than were most American girls of her period and her dignity on the platform of meetings is remembered. Her last years were stimulated by a project: the sale of alcohol to children in New Jersey had become a scandal and she proposed to stop it. It seems that her work was effective and that the women of other sects admired her. She has been somewhat wildly described as a religious maniac but what is known of her shows a fine mind trained in a formula.

But the child of her age was to have everything and be everything. She worried over him when he had troubles with algebra at school and his brilliance in other studies delighted her. For he was brilliant; the sensitive brain absorbed and recorded swiftly; he seemed to learn without effort and his memory of words was prodigious. A boy of fourteen who can use "irascible," "pyrotechnic," "impartial" and "memorial" correctly in an impromptu essay written for a prize of a quarter between two hot games of baseball is not as other American boys of fourteen. He had a passion for outlandish words and even invented one, a verb "higgle." It appears that to higgle is to behave in the manner of a school teacher. . . .

Baseball was now more important than verbs. The game had crystallized by advertisement and professional playing into the national sport and nuisance. Stephen's thin fingers began to thicken at the

knuckles. Being fifteen he wrote to Wallis McHarg
that he was going to be a professional ball player.
"But ma says it's not a serious occupation and Will
says I have to go to college first." Wallis, aged
sixteen, was sympathetic but wrote from Chicago
that Stephen had better go to college. There was an
alternative measure. Why should not Wallis and
Stephen enlist in the army? That would end all
difficulties with mothers and so forth. But baseball
had driven out war from Stephen's imagination and
he hung about taller boys playing on the beach and
endured the fate of umpires willingly if he might
be let in for an inning. Before he was sent off to
boarding school he had a sort of small fame in Asbury Park and thereabouts: no one could pitch a
ball that he would not catch barehanded.

Baseball made him eminent in the Hudson River
Institute at Claverack, New York. He arrived there
in February of 1887 with six pipes which he smoked
with some uneasiness and several volumes of Harry
Castleman's romances. The school was in high
repute at the time and was semi-military but, cu-
riously, the child who had once been fascinated by
the image of war could not drill well. He had
turned into a wiry lad whose mouth rose at the corners in a charming, remembered grin when he was
amused. Some of the boys thought him sullen because he seldom talked but baseball answered for
the social defect and there was enough muscle on

his long arms to get him safely through an immense fight in the spring of 1888. The fight began with Stephen's assertion that Lord Tennyson's poems were "swill." He lost a bit of a front tooth in making good his opinion.

His schooldays were to stay in mind with fragrance although, "I never learned anything there. American private schools are not as bad as our public schools, perhaps, but there is no great difference. I tried to learn French because my mother thought it important but no foreign language will ever be my friend. . . . But heaven was sunny blue and no rain fell on the diamond when I was playing baseball. I was very happy, there."

The summer of 1888 was happy with a new excitement. He went to work for his brother Townley, collecting items for Townley's press bureau at Asbury Park. The Jersey shore was populous, now, and fresh colonies sprang up along the endless beach. So a calamitous bicycle replaced the pony and Stephen ploughed along hot roads, hunting news of arrivals and departures and the small excitements of clambakes and sailing parties. A matron from Elizabeth was told, then, that "our papers" would be glad to know how long she was stopping at Avon-by-the-Sea and the *Philadelphia Press* accepted half a column on the history of a travelled merry-go-round which had come all the way from San Francisco to please the children of Asbury Park. The half column contains seven split infinitives. No earthly criticism could or ever did make Stephen Crane respect an infinitive. But he was now a reporter and the boys at Claverack were impressed by accounts of a gloveless prize fight seen secretly in a barn behind Atlantic City.

He met odd people; he saw, in the riff-raff of cheap entertainers and idlers, those amazing types who are still so feebly represented in American fiction, the attendants on shooting galleries and carrousels, the mercenary pilgrims of a tiny circus that broke up at Asbury. Stephen begged five dollars from his mother to start a lost cowboy back to Wyoming and the man gave him a real revolver alleged to have slain six Indians. A private education was in progress; it became plain that the world was a wide place filled with creatures who didn't conform to the rules prescribed for boys. And a Canadian lady, nameless in the record, gave him a paper bound copy of Count Tolstoy's "Sevastopol."

In February of 1890 a young civil engineer, Porter Cheney, was convalescent after typhoid in the house of a relative at Easton, Pennsylvania, where Lafayette College supplied what excitement there was. Cheney spent his afternoons in a poolroom behind a tobacco store and a lean, fair boy played pool very badly against him while they talked about camping trips in the New York hills and about

books. Cheney took his companion for some remarkable lounger who had no duties anywhere. At
times the boy fell abstracted and stood trying to
balance a cue on the small tip of his arched nose,
without much success. He burned cigarettes between the fingers of his left hand, seldom putting
them to his mouth, and asserted that Count Tolstoy
was the world's foremost writer. There was a lesser
fellow named Flaubert who had written a novel
much too long called "Salammbô." We are an-
nually told that "Salammbô" is a firework which
failed to explode but one wonders if that failure
was complete. Those catalogues of jewels, tribes,
gods and those terminal paragraphs in which the
view is switched so swiftly from one shape to a
thousand, from death to a setting sun or the sound
of something far away? If imitation is flattery, the
dead firework has been flattered. Well, he had read
"Salammbô" and did not think very well of the Car-
thaginian princess but this was better writing than
the English could do. No, he didn't like Robert
Louis Stevenson and he didn't know anything about
Henry James. The engineer was impressed, somehow, and described this lad to his sister in several
letters. The faculty of Lafayette remembered
Stephen as a tow-headed, pleasant boy who preferred
boxing to study. Stephen took home the pin of a
fraternity, Delta Upsilon, and in June of 1890 cap-

tained a mixed team of lads and grown men against a like team from Atlantic City. The score was 9 to 0 in Stephen's favour.

Summer of 1890 held other significant details in American civilization. Anthony Comstock, agent of the Society for the Suppression of Vice, invaded the shop of Eugene Caret, a new art dealer on Broadway, and bade him take from a show window the photograph of a statue by Rodin. M. Caret was so scared that he sold his stock and retired from New York City by the next liner. He was later bewildered to hear that the Metropolitan Museum had bought a copy of "L'Age d'Airan" and that it was public to any stare, without a figleaf, in the main court of the Museum. In July, Miss Frances Willard committed written mayhem on the person of Richard Watson Gilder for allowing the word "rape" to be printed in *The Century* because a magazine meant to be read by "Christian women" had no right to soil their eyes with such immundicities. Mr. Gilder carefully assured the great reformer that the American public was not wholly composed of susceptible Christian women but he got back no answer. Frances Willard had spoken and that was enough. In August, the editor of the *Atlantic Monthly* informed a young man in Topeka, Kansas, that "NewYork has now become the capital of art and letters in the United States." The issue of *Scribner's* for August contained "A Walk Up the Avenue" by Richard Harding Davis, already known as the author of "Galla-gher." Herewith, Davis mounted into celebrity as gracefully as he might have swung his fine body in its handsome dress to the cushions of a waiting cab. He rode, a figure of pleasant sophistication and fresh good humor, among passengers who lacked those qualities precisely and boys labouring with manu-script looked up and saw a star.

Townley Crane got for Stephen the post of corres-pondent to the *New York Tribune* in the town of Syracuse and Syracuse University was pleasant enough after Mrs. Crane consented to a change from engineering to "belles lettres." Stephen wanted to be a writer and his mother was willing. He must be good and always independent, always honest. She wrote these orders in one of her last letters. There was little left for Mary Crane but a trip to a congress of women in Boston, a few days of illness and a painless end in a hospital. Stephen would make for her kindness a small monument and would miss her silently.

He lounged at Syracuse in the back room of a restaurant and other freshmen were impressed by a classmate who sold sketches to the *Detroit Free Press* and who assured them that the police court was the most interesting place in Syracuse. He got notice from the faculty by telling a professor that he disagreed with Saint Paul's theory of sin and se-riously shocked the wife of another authority by de-

clining to meet Miss Frances Willard at her house
for the reason that he thought Miss Willard a fool.
A boy who had no reverence for sacred characters
must have been notable in a Methodist university
and spring made him famous. The baseball team
had never had such a shortstop and, after a vehement
argument, never so young a captain. It is legendary
that he was offered a place on a great professional
team but it is certain that his friends all knew Crane
was going to be a writer. Writing, he said, over
coffee and cigarettes in the restaurant, was a business
like any other. One trained one's mind to observe
and a man should be able to say something "worth
while" about any event. American writers were not
"sincere" and American magazines were "no good."
As for college it was a darned nuisance and he was
glad to be done with all things academic in June of
1891.

II

ROMANTIC MOVEMENTS

THERE was an old house on Twelfth Street which belonged, in 1891, to a rowdy Italian merchant who had adorned its big spaces to please an Irish dancer, and the union of such talent had produced a wonderful, gay result of gilded chairs and flaming tapestries in a drawing room that glowed, by night, under the jets of a monstrous chandelier. The flag of Ireland was effected in coloured tiles above the fireplace and elsewhere the house was quite as remarkable. But in September of 1891 this polychromatic paradise was rented to an invalid lady whose companion was an unsuccessful contralto, trained in Europe, a tall darkly pretty girl named Helen Trent.

Miss Trent left Avon, New Jersey, in the first week of September and came to rejoin the ailing Mrs. Potter. She found waiting a telegram from Avon: Stephen Crane was sorry that he had not seen Miss Trent to say good-bye. Miss Trent had an idea that this might be a silent boy who played baseball on the beach at Avon but she knew nothing of him and was

busy, nursing her friend's asthma and slowly pack-
ing for a journey to Switzerland.   Then on the tenth
a servant brought word that Mr. Crane was calling
and she went down to find a fair, untidy youth in
black clothes, whose eyes seemed brown in the glory
of the chandelier.

She thought him handsome, shy and dull.   The
call went on for warm, indifferent hours while she
tried to talk and he stared.   Then he startled her.
Had she seen Hamlin Garland, the new writer from
the West, while he lectured at Avon? [1]   She had not
but she asked what the Westerner looked like.

"Oh," Crane said, "like a nice Jesus Christ."

This was not in the conversational area of the year
1891.   The next morning Miss Trent had from Crane
a letter of a dozen sheets, written at the old Fifth
Avenue Hotel.   He was suddenly informative; his
brother Will had a baby named Helen; he was a reporter, himself; what was Miss Trent's favourite
color?   Did she like flowers and was she fond of
dogs?   He came, that night, to have these important
questions answered and kept coming, as the girl was
pleased by his slow talk of camping trips in Sullivan County and of curious people met on the Jersey
coast.   Then, one evening, he brought a terribly
bruised and plastered eye.   He had been sitting in
a saloon of the Bowery and a thrown bottle had
landed on him.   The accident did not amuse Miss

[1] See "A Son of the Middle Border."

Trent and she at once retired into the attitude of girls who find themselves comfortably older than admiring boys. Crane had already revealed some shocking opinions: a negro could be handsome, even without the "classic profile" demanded by a world soaked in the art of Leighton and Poynter: American religion was "mildewed": he found Buddhism interesting: he saw no reason why a young actress with a cottage at Avon couldn't go swimming at dawn, when the beach was empty, without a bathsuit. Miss Trent took the emphatic posture of American gentlewomen and forbade him to go near the Bowery. She had sung in charitable concerts, there, and it was a slum as vile as anything in Paris or Munich. It was not "nice" of Crane to go there. (The middle-aged lady who then was Helen Trent recalls her use of the word.) She spoke until Crane's lean body reared in his chair and he exploded with, "Hully gee!" The Bowery was the only interesting place in New York. Nobody had written anything "sincere" about its people. He was going to write a book some time soon about the Bowery and it was going to be a sincere book and he must see how these people lived and what they thought. Miss Trent broke in with protests. She was, for the hour, the composite portrait of all well-bred young women who have tried to explain proper art and letters to American artists. Why must he write any such book? Who wanted to read about such people? That Ferdinand Brunetière had lately stated, "The first temple of the young creative mind is the abyss," was not within her knowledge, nor within Crane's. So they wrangled unhappily and Crane walked out of the house, at last, leaving the word "hypocrite" in air. But he mailed a note, dated from the ferry to Jersey City: "I shall come back tomorrow night and we can start all over again. Yours sincerely, Stephen Crane."

So they argued and she sat playing Chopin for him at the black piano while he leaned on its side and sometimes hummed a barytone accompaniment to the wild bars. . . . He was enmeshed, one may guess, in an adventure that fell as fantastic on the mind of nineteen years spent in the lazy pleasantness of small towns and the placid medley of Asbury Park's crowded summer. The music pealed and chanted in this gaudy chamber where "great folds of lace swept down in orderly cascades . . . the colossal chandelier, gleaming like a Siamese headdress . . . caught subtle flashes from the gilt and tempestuous silk." He had seen handsome rooms, of course, in Newark and in Syracuse but he had never seen Latin profusion joined to Celtic vulgarity with a lovely girl in the pooled lights and colours, singing songs in the French that he could not read or understand. He was not unconscious, though, of the theatrical base in all this, for when she took him up to her guardian's boudoir of shrieking velvets and enamels, he asked, "When will the stage hands take it away?"

There seemed to be no cause for mention of her betrothed young surgeon, studying at Guy's Hospital in London, and Miss Trent was not wearing an engagement ring while she drove with Crane in the warm night through Central Park or when he took her to a play at Wallack's Theatre. They did not talk of books after a quarrel on the merits of Robert Louis Stevenson but she sewed a button on his coat and tried to make him brush the fair, limp hair back from the width of his forehead and he lighted her cigarettes although he did not then approve of these, for a lady. He was hoping for a place on the *Herald* and day after day he came to town and night after night he lounged on the piano, hearing the music of Chopin.

LAKEVIEW, N.J.
September 18, '91.

Dear Miss Trent:
I have found out something that you should know at once and will be up this evening to tell you.
Yours, S. C.

He came in solemnly excited. Did her guardian know that this house belonged to the very evil Mr. X. . . and that the Italian had furnished it for a "person"? Well, Mrs. Potter should take her away at once; people might not understand that the house was merely rented . . . Miss Trent woke up, honestly surprised and touched, with a lover on her hands. She thanked Crane and sent him away and, next evening, she was not at home. But the morning mail brought an undated scrawl on a leaf from a yellow notebook:

"Your window was lighted all last night but they said you were not in. I stood and looked at your window until a policeman came and made me go away. But I came back and looked until my head was just a sponge of lights. Please do not treat me like this. Nothing else counts but that."

It frightened her. He came on the evening of September twentieth while she was dressing to dine with friends in Sixtieth Street. Rain had fallen and Crane went out to find a hansom, then drove with her up the long channel of Fifth Avenue where white stone just patched the solid face of dim, chocolate buildings that rose above a pavement always blue under the lamps that sent, perhaps, jogging pulses of light on her bare arms. She remembers him quite silent as the hansom moved and when she came home late at night, he had left another note:

"You have the most beautiful arms I ever saw. You never should have to wear dresses with sleeves. If I could keep your arms nothing else would count. It would not matter if there was nothing else to hope for in the world or if there was no more world. In dreams, don't you ever fall and fall but not be afraid of anything because somebody safe is with you? I shall be here tomorrow. I must get back to Ed's house, now."

So he went off on the dreary trip to his brother Edmund's house at Lakeview, outside Paterson, where he was teaching lads of the neighbourhood to play tearing football on Saturdays and writing furiously through nights in an attic turned to a study for his use. He came back, on September 21st, and Miss Trent strolled nervously into the florid drawing room to tell him that she was to be married in London, soon. Crane gave a quick gasp and lifted both hands to his face. Then he spun and walked out of the house, permanently. In January of 1900, when an Englishman pointed out the celebrated Stephen Crane, she saw him across the flare of a London theatre without knowing why he was celebrated. But in "The Black Riders," on the eleventh page:

> "Should the wide world roll away,
> Leaving black terror,
> Limitless night,
> Nor God, nor man, nor place to stand,
> Would be to me essential,
> If thou and thy white arms were there,
> And the fall to doom a long way."

2

Another romantic movement had accomplished itself while Crane grew up. Three days before he

was born, sheriffs came to the house of William
Marcy Tweed, in New York, and tenderly put under
arrest the tall, obese stevedore who had stolen from
the city one hundred and fifty million dollars. His
fall was largely the act of a disgusted Irish gambler
and gelatinous grandees of New York sat in some
confusion while the trial was forced along by a young
Yankee lawyer. Many of the city's foremost men
had privately done Tweed's bidding and had publicly
shaken his gouty fingers while he lolled in his carriage
at the curb of Wall Street. But Tweed's fall advertised radiantly the wealth and rascality of the
plundered town's ruling strata and tiny journals in-
land printed with due exaggeration the list of his
pleasures and palaces. The tawdry seaport was
suddenly Babylon in the mouths of rural preachers
and dealers in pornography now shifted the scene of
revels from Boston or Philadelphia to New York.
The city's population swelled between 1871 and 1873
by a hundred thousand and of this earned increment
it was known that hundreds were people of means
who now gazed in real awe at the stiff, timid native
aristocrats. New York took on, in the nation's eye,
the combined aspect of an eating house and a gilded
lupanar irresistible to the peasant mind. There followed a gradual welding of the parochial rich with a
fresh plutocracy ready to outdo the pomps of the first
Belmont and soon the child of this match was a glittering amalgam which, toward 1890, complied with

the custom of all adolescents and fell in love with itself.

Metropolitan society of the nineteenth century's last decade had a colour of compound paradox. It was metropolitan only in location; it viewed with amazing disdain the aristocracies of other cities and instead of drawing in their wealth and fashion it ignored them. It was plainly a society of capital for it permitted family after family once eminent to sink from its midst unable to endure the monetary strain of entertainment. Yet it clung with ferocity to Washington Irving's pleasant myth of a Knickerbocker lordship while the descendants of the real Patroons quietly took themselves elsewhere or fell into humdrum obscurity as the high world became a grocer's window filled with quarrelsome fruit. Money talked so loudly that small satirists of "Puck" and "Life" were not deceived by the grand gesticulations of the aged Ward McAllister and the younger Berry Wall. The man in the street knew that descent had the least possible part in this feckless, handsome show. But the whole movement was ruled by a sickly æstheticism: these vulgarians went labouring and stumbling after a dim ideal. They hunted grace.

This grace was altogether external and pictorial. A movement somewhat similar was afoot in France and England, the available models, where capitalism wooed a real aristocracy and wedded it effectively

with all the blessings of journalism on the tinselled
bed.   In meek rapture from afar the ruling women
of New York could observe the impatient gaieties
of the Prince of Wales and might imitate with feeble
discretion the balls of Madame de Sagan.   "Anglo-
mania" was nothing more than a rather wavering
effort to improve the American picture.   Now, anti-
quaries found a market for chairs of stale oak and
tapestries that might be Gobelins were carted to
new country houses—some of which, strangely, were
discovered to have long been owned by their pos-
sessors.   Meanwhile, gold service flashed at dinners
given to successive French painters who pronounced
American women the loveliest of earth.   In 1896 it
was seen with delight that eighty ladies appeared
crowned with jewels in the boxes of the Opera and in
1897 one of them offered to remit the rents of certain
cottagers beside her park on Long Island if they
would let her replace the tin of roofs with English
thatch.   But the American winds blew the thatch
away. . . .

Men were seldom powerful in this scented herd
but there did tower one commanding female shape.
Documents well display the alert and vigorous Caroline, wife and then widow of William Astor, a woman
truly charitable who could conceive a gay and liberal
grouping of her allies.   She so far ruled the mani-
fold fluctuations of her tribe that when old McAllister mentioned "our social leader" housewives of the

midlands knew just who was meant. If rivals did not concede that she was absolute, the baser world did, and she addressed herself in the third person to editors of newspapers. It was reported that she was subtle, wise in the mysteries of arts and crafts, and it is true that she would verbally singe a committee for the stupid adornment of a public hall, but she would not permit the same committee to consult John La Farge because the colourist was a "professional painter." She liked to laugh, but she made known her surprise that her son should go to dine with Mark Twain. She was an admirer of Ouida and read "Moths" five times, so she must have been literate, yet, hearing that Miss Alice Duer had begun to publish poems, she cried, "But the girl's not at all plain!" and seated in London beside Harold Frederic she found the novelist amusing, so was moved to ask who were his friends?

"Mostly writers and artists."

"Indeed," said Mrs. Astor, after a musing period, "that must be very strange!"

She lived on until she could be described in a popular romance as an old, old lady drowsing on a golden throne but when she died and appraisers were busy with her goods, an astonished public read that the chairs of her ballroom might have been owned by any one and that the carpet of her famous, dreaded staircase, threadbare and faded, had no more a value.

If all critical elements are carefully shorn from a society by the will of its rulers, it can remain comfortably in love with its own flesh, and it did. The smart world of New York's great decade failed to discover in the patronage of its superiors, the last flavour of aristocratic contempt. In those bright rooms, agitated for weeks by the assertion, without exhibition, of fresh rosebuds pinned to the garters of young beauty, where were hung pictures by Rembrandt alongside the trash of Marcus Stone and Debat-Ponsin, the native artists, the native critics had no place. It was understood that they existed, probably somewhere in the shadowy void where vague hordes were known to be crying out for the abolition of wine, wealth and unwedded love. But a great lady phrased the objection of her group quite neatly in 1897 to a travelling Briton: "On the whole, Sir William, don't you think that reformers and writers always make things unpleasant?" And a little later William Dean Howells was driven to muse: "It sometimes seems to me that the wealthy class of New York fights shy of the writer and artist just as a schoolboy is timid before an older man. This was not true of Boston. Mrs. James Fields and a dozen other intelligent women were more than hospitable. . . . A young writer in New York may be given tea and a bun by his publisher's wife but the city is not hospitable to talents unless they come from Europe. Nor is the European artist always welcome. . . . You asked me last year what the rich New Yorker reads. He reads the newspapers." Precisely. If the Narcissus read anything, it read the newspapers and its whole notion of things came from that unsubstantial, flashy medium. The paradox was perfect: a society bragged of its isolate refinement and its ideas were those of the street. So in 1903 an acidulous Russian Ambassador noted that New York's high world was "une servante qui porte assez gauchement les robes de sa dame" and the same Count Cassini also wrote that the matrons of the city had not heard of the printing press save as an instrument to list "their stupid names."

Who doubts that such an attitude was profoundly influential? The wealthy class of the nation's largest city was a natural mark for imitation. The capital of arts and letters had no welcome for the artist, native or foreign, unless he had been stamped by the press, its guide, as an eminence. He was permitted to exist upon such terms as he could make with his environment and a realm of cheap lodgings, cheap restaurants and cheap journals lay ready to provide that environment unless he had cash in pocket to keep him elsewhere. For another romantic movement was afoot: the romance of journalism as the school of letters was well established, now, and the delusion brought boys scurrying to the offices of the New York papers in droves. Had not Richard Harding Davis, Julian Ralph, Edward

Townsend and, more brilliantly still, Rudyard Kipling emerged from that battering apprenticeship? So journalism took hold of the national fiction and for a decade fiercely attuned it to the key of commonplace perceptions and to the flattery of an inferior city.

The tone of the press, in the decade of this history, was flattering to all things visible in New York save administration as contrived by the Democratic party. Spasmodically, in the cramped critical departments of the *Sun* or *The Herald,* a Mayo Hazeltine or Charles Meltzer might cry against some popular novel or deride the cult of suave goddesses shoved forward by the Frohmans and Palmers in banal rotation on the stages of Broadway. Everybody could see, though, that these were the gruntings of discontented and sour critics. The word "critic" itself was rather shunned. The word "reviewer" was brought into being; it was a milder, more pleasant generality. One reviewed the spectacle of the city's superb existence and was thrilled by such immensities of life and colour. Manhattan became a crowned woman in the frescoes of new hotels and if James Huneker, in the pages of a perky monthly called *Mdlle. New York,* chose to hint that Manhattan really resembled a customs-house clerk, why, his magazine had its reward and did not live long. If *The Arena* kept insisting that the public schools were abominable and that the public libraries were maladministered antiques, the audience of Flower's dull ravings was mostly made up of schoolteachers and reformers. Meanwhile, the show was good. Victor Herbert's increased orchestras made silky melody in theatres where shoulders were naked at last, after the long discussion of a gentlewoman's right to dress as she pleased. Each autumn the groomed horses trotted in the New Madison Square Garden, after football games had filled New York with roarings and with the sight of youth pouring down to the festival with chrysanthemums in its coat of tawny English cloth. Each winter the Opera dazzled provincials and some people listened to the voices of the De Reszkés, of the soft eyed Schalchi, of the patrician Emma Eames. These things were popular and therefore good and the newspapers reported them in affable detail never smirched by realism. The Sunday supplement was invented and suburban householders could see in hazy photographs the very bathrooms of the obliging rich who also let heaped gifts at the weddings of their daughters appear for the contemplation of brides who were not American beauties plucked by European noblemen from the profitable stem. All brides were ravishing and all weddings gorgeous in that strange decade, just as all parades of militia and all civic ceremonies were "inspiring sights." The Narcissus tilted a mirror to his visage and beamed with condescension on an envious land.

It is plain that this pervasive flattery must have been, in some part, due to ignorance and to a lack of any valuing sense. But that its root was the congenital cowardice of the educated American there can be no doubt at all. A movement in counterpoint was sounding in the magazines, new and old. The whole history of the decade's mild revolt against the quality of American life is bound for display in the slick paper of *The Century, Harper, Scribner's, McClure's* and *The Cosmopolitan*, revived under John Walker to startle editors by its mad varieties. Revolt showed first in the illustrations which swung out of the inane traditional woodcuts and dreary imitations of Maclise into the stony veracities of Howard Pyle and the smooth skill of Joseph Pennell and of Radford Brennan, Pennell's superior in draughtsmanship, his inferior in assemblage. People suddenly looked like people, it was said, and if the general taste hung to the domestic pleasantness of Charles Gibson and Howard Christy, there were other hands at work. Here was Abbey's feathery line. Here were Low, Linson, Sonntag, Castaigne, and the earlier Maxfield Parrish. Peter Newell and A. B. Frost made farces of the respectable commoner's clothes and his face took on a satiric emptiness under their touch. Here, little noticed, were the photographic exactitudes of Ernest Peixotto and Jay Hambidge. Taste moved forward boldly and a children's monthly, *St. Nicholas*, offered derivations from the art of Georges Seurat to a public which, like that of his own country, had never heard of him.

In this pictorial progress *The Century* had taken the lead and it now led on in a new venture. There began to be a mild, most courteous analysis of the American scene and Richard Gilder bravely introduced, through his magazine, essayists and historians whose work was not devised to flatter any element of the nation. He had already made himself responsible for an impartial history of the Civil War and he was a man of defined political tendencies. The cloudy stir to be christened "the reform movement" found an ally in him and he conciliated intellectual groups by critical matter far outside the general taste. But the charming intelligence of the man was haunted by some barren theory of good form. He would allow the honorable studies of Walter Wyckoff, those first visions of the American labourer, to pass from his desk to the office of *Scribner's* because "The Workers" seemed flamboyant and he shrank from Josiah Flynt's sketches in crime because their subjects were "sordid." It is uncanny that Gilder, first of the native editors, should have recognized the talent of Jack London, as he did. The success of *McClure's Magazine*, with its profanity, its bad poems and its vivacity, passed his understanding but he made of *The Century* a stable, enduring creature and its life is not yet spent.

These editorial powers, with their growing public, knew that eyes were turned to the artistic whirlpool of the European world. They saw that publishers found profit in translations of Zola. Some plane of the United States was soothed and saddened by Loti's wailing grace. There was an outcry against unwholesome foreign fiction and even Rudyard Kipling, already sacred, was now and then attacked. But in the midst of these noises, Howells and his local rival, Mayo Hazeltine, praised Russian writing and implored their admirers to read Thomas Hardy. Was there, then, something viable in the mode that Hazeltine had named "Stark realism"? There might be and one can follow, in that decade, two parallel motions. There was the glib, smoothly moving fiction of the reportorial school and there was a minor realism by permission, under surveillance. This realism was hedged and neatly confined both by editorial policy and by the temper of its friends. Howells was its father and it stayed well within his orbit, daring little and effecting not much more than a break with the moralities and prettiness of that precedent fiction which has left the single name of Bret Harte, an artist of whom it has been surprisingly discovered since his death that he imitated Dickens, quite as though Harte's critics while he lived had not noticed the habit. Harte's influence, too, survived in this quasi-realism. The neat pattern of his product had stamped itself too heavily in the editorial brain, where it persists. But intermittently arrived in print stories of commonplace people and the public welcomed this placid observation of sempstresses soured by age, of bored country women, of dirty stokers in Pennsylvania mills. The observation was commonplace as were the themes. Here were dignity and sincerity, with Hamlin Garland's western sketches and Sarah Jewett's acid etchings to add some genuine, memorable achievements in brief narrative.

Yet here came a boy whose visual sense was unique in American writing and whose mind by some inner process had stripped itself of all respect for those prevalent theories which have cursed the national fiction. He was already an ironist, already able to plant his impressions with force and reckless of the consequent shock to a public softened by long nursing at the hands of limited men. Upon what section of the visible scene would he commence his sardonic operations? Perhaps it was simple recoil from the lukewarm current of letters, or perhaps it was a deeper curiosity that took Stephen Crane headlong and resolute into the slums.

III

MAGGIE: A GIRL OF THE STREETS

NEW YORK was proud of the Bowery precisely as a child is proud of a burned thumb and the fame of the long, tawdry street grew by rumours of incredible debauchery until in 1890 one Ahearn, a publican, found it worth his while to post youths in the Grand Central Station who offered arriving men to "Show you the Bowery for a dollar, mister?" with the understanding that trips through the glamorous sink would end in supper at Ahearn's saloon where ruffians duly arranged battles among the tables and prizefighters were bred. But there was nothing fictitious in the poverty of the region and the soberly industrious Continental Jews who would finally tame the quarter by mere numbers were still in a passive minority. The name "Bowery" had been made inclusive: all adjoining streets, alleys and squares held Bowery boys and Bowery girls in popular report. The alleys, too, were plentiful and buildings of wood crazily leaned above fissures black by night, as part of the Democratic revenues rose from the profit of lighting and cleaning small lanes which were never lighted and so seldom cleaned that corpses often were unearthed in piles of rubbish months after their relatives had given up a hunt for some vanished entity. The Bowery's self had an honest average of three saloons to the block and its nightly glitter raked the eye with raw tones of green and red in the glazed doors of these solacing haunts. Laborious prostitutes strolled from sunset to dawn on selected beats and many moved westward from the economy of lodgings on Third Avenue to the public halls of Broadway and Fourteenth Street.

The Bowery, though, was funny. Comedians aped its dress on the stage of Koster and Bial's improper vaudeville and speakers at banquets recited Bowery jokes. There was no other slum in America so settled of speech and habit. It was supposed that the Bowery invented words. In 1890 the word "jay" was current as a Bowery coinage in contemptuous reference. The word was actually from the south, of course, and its original employment was the sentence, "Naked as a jaybird," much used by begging tramps who spent the warm season in the north. Patches of English slang floated in the talk of the district and blossomed as native when reporters drew on this reservoir of unchaste diction. Stephen Crane found "on the turf" a convenient evasion of "prostitute," for instance, and was accused of inventing a meaning known in London before 1870. But the Bowery language was humorous, as are a dozen dialects in which the fierce, defensive cynicism of the illiterate American takes on colour and shape. There was a choppy rhythm in the speech from which the sound of "th" had been drawn away. Many vowels were washed over so briskly that it took experience to tell whether they had been pronounced at all by some hasty group of lads hanging for a breath together while the policeman's back was turned. For the Bowery was full of youth that lived without license to draw pay and the poor preyed comfortably on the poor.

In January of 1892, Wallis McHarg came to New York, ready to sail for Germany and the study of medicine. He found Crane's address by way of the *New York Herald's* office and invaded a house of far East 23rd Street where Crane was sharing the big bedroom of some young actor.[1] At once Wallis must be shown the Bowery and Crane led his friend down its reaches with a happy air of proprietorship. Here was the saloon where he had got a black eye. This was the dance hall wrecked by a gang of sailors from the Brooklyn Navy Yard who had been wrongfully expelled. There was a notorious procurer and that girl was supposed to be the daughter of a wealthy family somewhere uptown who came here for the curious pleasure of attracting suitors and then making them quarrel while she went to refuge in the

[1] Probably William Riley Hatch.

shadow of some policeman. Then Crane abruptly said, "I want you to read my book."

McHarg had no pretentions in letters. He was the very practical son of a roaming family, not much given to reading. He took the pile of manuscript to his room at the Gilsey House and looked through its neat, tall writing with bewilderment. No character had a name in the short story of a girl seduced by a bartender and the use of "God damn!" struck him as impossibly accurate. Here was something strange, new and outlandish. Next day he told Crane that nobody would print such a story and that the people should have names. And when had Crane written this?

"I wrote it in two days before Christmas," said Crane, coolly, and then admitted that his brother William also thought the people must have names. The lawyer had seen the defect of the experiment. These characters stirring in a stupid mist and almost without physical being, would confuse readers. They were "the girl," "the girl's mother," her brother, her lover and out of this original framework something remains. The "woman of experience and audacity" was never thereafter christened.

McHarg went off to Germany appalled and thrilled. He had read the curt, compressed tales of the Wyoming Valley which Crane sent him in clippings from the *New York Tribune* but he had never taken "Stevie" seriously as an author bound to be famous. Now the younger boy had done something that was at least extraordinary and would create noise if anybody published it. Late in February he had a note, dateless and without address. Brother William had named the book. It was now "Maggie: A Girl of the Street," and in a postscript, "The *Herald* fired me last week."

Crane's shadowy term with the *New York Herald* exactly prophesied his whole career as a journalist. He could not report. Apparently he did not even try to report. Of what use to any newspaper was an impression of impatient horses kicking "grey ice of the gutter into silvery angles that hurtled and clicked on frozen stone" when the boy had been sent to get the facts of a large and important fire? The stamping horses hitched to the engine and the stolid movement of a young fireman stepping back from a falling wall, these things took his eye and went on paper. The name of the building's owner, its number on the street and the question of its insurance simply wafted from the brain behind the plunging blue eyes. Nor could a city editor accept an interview with a prominent alderman when that dignitary, under charges of corruption, "sat like a rural soup tureen in his chair and said, 'Aw!' sadly whenever ash from his cigar bounced on his vest of blood and black." It is not now to be proved that the *Herald* discharged Crane. He was probably taken to task for some fantasy on an alderman or an actress and dismissed himself.

But a boy of twenty, loose in the world filled with improvident and hopeful other boys, would not much care, and "Maggie" was ready for high inspection. Crane got himself a note of introduction from his brother Townley and appeared at the offices of *The Century*. Richard Watson Gilder knew all the Cranes and knew that this must be young Stephen before he read the note. "He was thin and his blue eyes seemed enormous. He sat wrapped in a grey ulster much too big for him, talking very slowly about his family with whom I had lost touch," Gilder wrote, later. "I saw that his manuscript was not long and gave him an appointment for the next day."

Gilder had a bad evening with "Maggie." The novel is almost unknown to Americans. It begins: "A very little boy stood upon a heap of gravel for the honour of Rum Alley. He was throwing stones at howling urchins from Devil's Row who were circling madly about the heap and pelting him. His small body was writhing in the delivery of great, crimson oaths. . . . From a window of an apartment house that upreared its form from amid squat, ignorant stables, there leaned a curious woman. . . . The engineer of a passive tugboat hung lazily to a railing and watched. Over on the Island, a worm of yellow convicts came from the shadow of a grey ominous building and crawled slowly along the river's

brink. . . ."   The calm world watches Jimmie Johnson fight and then he goes home to his drunken
mother, with his drunken father.   His sister Maggie
upbraids him: "Yeh knows it puts mudder out
when yehs comes home half dead, an' it's like we'll
all get a poundin'."   To this unsentimental address,
Jimmie answers, "Ah, what de hell!   Shut up or I'll
smack yer' mout', see?"

These children grow up in the shade of
fear.   Their mother is an incessant drinker who bul-
lies them.   Jimmie becomes a truck driver invested
by habit with an awful contempt for everything,
especially those strings of street cars that followed
his truck "like intent bugs."   He has some respect for
heavy fire engines: "They had been known to overturn street cars.   Those leaping horses, striking
sparks from the cobbles in their forward lunge, were
creatures to be ineffably admired.   The clang of the
gong pierced his breast like a noise of remembered
war."   He attends meetings in missions where the
hearers, hopeful only of free soup, confuse the
preacher with Christ.   He "menaced mankind at the
intersection of streets . . . dreaming blood-red
dreams at the passing of pretty women."   He se-
duces a pair of women, himself, who "caused him
considerable annoyance by breaking forth simulta-
neously, at fateful intervals, into wailings about support, marriage and infants. . . . Nevertheless, he
had on a certain starlit evening, said wonderingly

and quite reverently: "Deh moon looks like hell, don't it?"

His sister Maggie is a pretty girl—Crane did not describe her—who goes to work for a Jew in a collar factory at five dollars a week rather than go on the streets. She is wooed by Pete, an opulent young bartender who hasn't the slightest thought of marrying her and does not when he wearies of her stupid prettiness and goes back to a more experienced mistress. Jimmie has vague fancies that his own position should not permit him to be too stern with Maggie—there are his own informal brides—but all his ideas are cribbed by the conservatism of his breed. He allows his mother to turn Maggie out and in a chapter unforgettable the feeble child goes drifting across New York, trying to speak to busy men, and halts in the profound shadow of the river's edge. Word being brought that "Mag's dead" her mother finishes supper before breaking into due lamentations and, urged on by friends, concludes the story with the cry, "Oh, yes, I'll fergive her! I'll fergive her!" and the first ironic novel ever written by an American thus crisply ends.

On his own admission, made in 1904, this book gave Richard Gilder a fearful shock. It seemed to him daring and filled with good touches but it was "cruel." There was no visible sentiment. These creatures of an environment had no tenderness and no restraint of action to excuse their callosity and, next day, Gilder sat pointing out excessive adjectives and slaughtered infinitives to the shy boy who finally cut him short with an untactful question: "You mean that the story's too honest?"

Being a gentleman as well as an editor Gilder gave his courteous little nod and "Maggie" was carried away from him in a pocket of the grey ulster. It may have consoled Crane, on March 23rd, 1892, that Gilder saw nothing obscene in the story. There is no animal detail in the seduction of Maggie Johnson and the profanity of the novel was simply the "damns" and "curse yehs" of the Bowery's emotion lamely piling out. But Crane here had his first experience, without guessing, of a dualism which faces all American writers. In two years more Gilder would be bidding his friends to read the English Arthur Morrison's "Tales of Mean Streets" and would be aiding the Tenement Commission to clean up the slums of New York. But that a story of those slums, told without apology, should appear in *The Century* of 1892 was unthinkable. In 1904 he was asked why Morrison's "Child of the Jago" did not offend him when "Maggie" still seemed a breach of taste and he made response: "But Mr. Morrison's an Englishman!" as if some permission of God rested on the Briton that his truculent realisms should be found inoffensive. The attitude might be comic if it were still not spinal in American editors of the year 1923.

"Maggie" roamed the offices of various magazines in March and April until Crane locked her up in a box at his brother Edmund's house in New Jersey and got to work on sketches which he might sell to the *New York Tribune.* He was now a freelance reporter, one of hundreds who haunted Park Row daily, trying to sell interviews with notables, articles investigatory and descriptive. The *Tribune* was a good market; he was known favourably in the office and the paper had printed his work since 1888. Now he began to have a little reputation in all the offices, before summer. His adjectives were oddly placed and his brusque paragraphs stayed in the mind. To say that an injured streetsweeper, "Flattened his face toward heaven and sent up a jet of violet, fastidious curses," was certainly too elaborate for the journalism of 1892 but men buying material for the *Sun* and *Tribune* would remember even when they had chopped it from an account of an accident in Twenty Third Street.

Meanwhile, the boy was engaged in a private game. He was being independent, as his mother had ordered him to be, and small pay, cheap rooms, casual food were part of the sport. If he sat by night on a bench in Union Square with John Northern Hilliard or Acton Davies wondering when a check might drop from somewhere, there was pleasure in that and Hilliard could tell him stories about the West. If the check was too long in coming, he could get on a train and go to Lakeview where he spent aimless evenings with pretty girls singing popular songs around a piano.   In May he wandered through Syracuse and glanced at the class of 1894, then spent a week at Port Jervis with William Crane.   But on May 26th, some check had been too long delayed and he wrote to Acton Davies that he must have five dollars before he went to Lakeview or Edmund Crane's front door and his baby would be his next meal.   The baby and the door survived.   In June he admitted that he had sat on his brother's back steps and compiled a mental dictionary of oaths.   In July he was in Asbury Park, once more, sending off sketches to the *Tribune* and helping Townley Crane gather notes of a very busy season.

The season was also busy in the *Tribune's* offices. Whitelaw Reid was candidate for vice president on the Republican ticket and the early campaign went badly although William McKinley had been brought east to speak on protection of industries from New Hampshire to Virginia.   Reid's newspaper shows the strain of operation in behalf of a losing issue.   Every meeting of workers that showed favour to the Republican party was reported in fullest detail.   It was understood that the Grand Army of the Republic inclined toward Harrison and Reid and the Army's encampments fill page on page of the paper.   Various societies of the labouring class, as it began to be

called, had outings and holidays on the Jersey shore.
Reports of these doings, then, were waited on eagerly
in Park Row.

Meanwhile Crane lounged about Asbury and Avon
and played baseball rather less than formerly. Some
of his old friends thought he looked unwell, that
summer, and his silences were prolonged. He was a
little criticized for an article on Asbury Park in
which the respectable fathers of respectable families
were sweepingly mentioned as beings "with a watch
chain and about three children apiece." Then, one
day, his brother went to a funeral in Newark and
left the impressionist to chronicle a parade. These
good men lugged banners praising Harrison and Reid
and Crane, looking at the motion of this spectacle,
forgot that Reid owned the *New York Tribune*.
He merely saw a number of sweating persons who
mostly worked with their hands, marching on behalf
of capital and the thing amused him. All parades
were silly, anyhow, and this was too silly. The men
shambled in dust and sunlight for his eye. There
was a doubled oversight both at the press bureau
in Asbury and in the office of the paper on Park Row.
Next week complaints arrived at the *Tribune's* door
on every mail. The paragraph, printed obscurely
and in only one edition, was too much read. Crane
had fallen foul of the American commoner's inalien-
able right to be reported respectfully, no matter how

tawdry or foolish his communal manifestations may appear. Somebody[1] in Park Row sent Townley Crane a heated message and Stephen retired to Port Jervis, to ride a horse in peace. The emotions of Townley Crane are now inscrutable.

But "Maggie" was haunting her maker. In November, Crane borrowed one thousand dollars from his brother William and went to New York with the revised manuscript. He had a definite scheme: cheap publishing houses then often put out paper-bound novels at the author's expense and since the higher criticism would have none of "Maggie" let her be seen on the newstands. Few of his friends had read the manuscript and he knew, now, that Stephen Crane was nobody at all in the city of New York: "I hunted a long time for some perfectly commonplace name . . . I think that I asked (Post) Wheeler what he thought was the stupidest name in the world. He suggested Johnson or Smith and Johnston Smith went on the ugly yellow cover of the book by mistake. You see, I was going to wait until all the world was pyrotechnic about Johnston Smith's 'Maggie' and then I was going to flop down like a trapeze performer from the wire and, coming forward with all the modest grace of a consumptive nun, say, I am he, friends! . . . The bill for printing eleven hundred copies was $869 and Appleton's tell me that the printer must have made about $700 out of me.

[1] Whitelaw Reid was not responsible.

. . . A firm of religious and medical printers did me the dirt. You may take this as proffered evidence of my imbecility. Will made me get the thing copyrighted. I had not even that much sense."

He was obliged to sign a statement that he was twenty-one years old before this vanished firm would take the contract. They refused their name for the titlepage, in any case.[1] But "Maggie" was now born in mustard paper with the price "50 cents" on the right hand upper corner of the cover and the talent of Johnston Smith might be seen by the world if Stephen Crane could get somebody to expose it for sale. So the book was offered to the shops which in that year were quietly selling flat, large copies of Emile Zola's "La Terre" and "Potbouillie" to schoolboys. But nobody would take "Maggie" save Brentano's which took a dozen copies and returned ten of them. The newstands didn't want such a book. By the end of January, 1893, Crane had got rid of a hundred "Maggies" and on one of these, sold in 1922 for two hundred and fifty dollars, is the inscription, "Miss Wortzmann. This story will not edify or improve you and may not even interest you but I owe your papa $1.30 for tobacco. S. Crane." So "Maggie" lay in yellow piles in the corners of his room and Crane went into that period of starvation so much admired in the history of artists by comfortable critics, sure of next week's bread.

[1] The name of this firm seems to be lost forever.

His family knew nothing about this. When he dropped down to Edmund's house at Lakeview he was as usual, ready to play games with his small nieces and likely to write all night, coming to breakfast when the small household was at lunch. The secrecy of a boy was heavy in him; he had the icy courage of a sensitive nature which has taught itself to be brave; Edmund was under orders never to lend him more than five cents at a time. But one night there was not enough in his pocket to get him to Lakeview and he tramped through the mud of a country road, dazed with emptiness, with the sense of a great bundle pressing on his back. Then some man said from frosty shadow, "You seem to be in a pretty bad way, boy," and took hold of his arm. Crane mumbled that he was ill and they tramped toward Lakeview together, the countryman drawling out some wandering yarn, until Crane saw the lamps of his brother's house. The farmer shook hands with him and trudged away, his face unseen, to become the twelfth chapter of "The Red Badge of Courage."

Crane's courage afterwards seemed to him simple silliness. Two of his brothers believed in his talent and their homes were his. He could have given himself quarters with William or Edmund and stayed as a pensioner until, somehow, he had established himself with a public. But Crane's independence had a bent almost savage and ungracious. He would not tell his family anything about gloomy days in the old building of the Art Students' League in East Twenty Third Street and there was a new biting horror; he could not write, now. Not only could he not write enough wooden descriptions of fires and strikes in Brooklyn—temporarily the home of strikes—to pay his meals but he could write nothing that pleased his own judgment. All words seemed false and awkward. One day in February he came to Edmund's office in New York and said, drearily, "I'll trouble you for five cents, Ed" and on the first of March he answered an advertisement in the *Herald* and became clerk in a wholesale house on Bleecker Street for one week, precisely.

The external Stephen Crane of this passage was a silent boy who might be spurred on to amuse the crowd in a lamentable restaurant of lowest Lexington Avenue. Here the waiters wiped spoons in the leather pockets of fouled aprons and here Crane might rouse himself to say that Mark Twain's "Yankee in King Arthur's Court" was "inappropriate as a drunken bride." The quality of his talk was tinctured always by adjectives strange and prolonged. His boarding house was a respectable hypocrite of a place. An ancient egg had a "snarling smell." The feather on the Sunday hat of a pretty chambermaid was "quivering invitation."

This pretty chambermaid was named Jennie Creegan and all the crew of hapless youths whose beds

she made called her Bunny. She sat on trunks,
chewing gum "like a slim, reminiscing cow" and told
tales of the Bowery. Crane had borrowed of her
some phrases of "Maggie" and she tried to read the
book when he gave her a copy but the words were
too hard. One day she collected an armfull of
"Maggies" from Crane's quarters and used them to
light a fire. The ironist grinned and helped her to
lug the dusty books downstairs.

Hamlin Garland appeared in this fog as the rescu-
ing angel. Crane was surrounded by other boys,
some younger than himself, who partly understood
that "Maggie" was a rare performance. When any-
one praised him with intelligence, he might flush and
beam but nobody in authority had yet said good
words of "Maggie" and perhaps his confidence was
slipping when Mr. Garland wrote to him inviting a
call. The handsome Westerner was living not too
comfortably in Harlem and Crane tramped the four
miles between their rooms for the first visit. Mr.
Garland was startled by the boy's admission that he
would give away his literary future for thirty dollars
and began work with an instant, practical kindness.
So a copy of "Maggie" was sent to William Dean
Howells. Sketches were mailed to O. B. Flower of
the *Arena* and Flower promptly bought "An
Ominous Babe" for twenty-five dollars. The ad-
viser understood something of markets. He recommended Crane to *The Press,* fed him beefsteak

and loaned him dollars. This was no springtide of
fortune but it was something solid after a winter of
freezing doubts and *The Press* had literary preten-
sions second just to those of the glittering and eclec-
tic *Sun*. To Garland there was already a tragic
vesture on this lean, sallow boy, who had played baseball with him at Avon eighteen months before. The
palpitating eyes were sombre; the tearing intensity
of the brain was clear to his experience. He might
laugh a little when Crane hummed tuneless anthems
in praise of food but, to his scrutiny, Crane was a
shape of pathos.

Crane's appearance misled people. He had heavy
shoulders and a pair of meagre hips that made clothes
fit him badly even when he dressed with care. His
eyes discoloured easily and, after a night of work or
indifferent poker, he seemed always ill. Women invariably thought him handsome; men, with some
exceptions, thought his face too long and his mouth
too flexible. But even in the summer of 1893 after
weeks of good diet at Edmund Crane's house he left
an impression of starved neglect on strangers. As
this narrative must be, in part, the demolition of a
romantic myth, it should be pointed out that Crane
was actually muscular and his body was an enduring
machine that could carry him through a good deal of
fatigue, as long as he was given plenteous sleep. But
his exterior was, somehow, fantastic and already, in
March of 1893, he was pointed out to a Southerner,

Ford Bemis, as an eccentric who spent all his time in dives of the Bowery and was the outcast son of an Episcopal bishop. It should be pointed out, too, that Crane had a degree of the grand innocence in his character. Walking across Union Square with Elbert Hubbard and Acton Davies, he would deliberately stop to talk to an interesting tramp or some elderly painted woman and would hold his circumspect, annoyed companions still until the wearisome string of lies had been rolled out. "He had," said Hubbard, "no sense of propriety." The publisher's own exterior was that of a professional Bohemian from the novels of Mürger, but he was circumspect in the highest degree and Crane's simmering curiosity frightened him.

Meanwhile William Dean Howells had gone sedately mad over "Maggie" and was trying to persuade Henry Harper to have the book issued with more dignity. Harper declined but Howells asked Crane to dine with him and the impressionist appeared—in John Hilliard's best suit—to get a dose of praise administered by the first critic of the land. Howells happened to be master of a small art that is not forgotten: he could stand in a crowd and make compliments without embarrassing the beneficiary or annoying the witnesses. He presented Crane to his other guests with, "Here is a writer who has sprung into life fully armed," and followed that music by saying, while Mark Twain was under discussion,

"Mr. Crane can do things that Clemens can't."
Then, after dinner, he took down the volume of
Emily Dickinson's poems and read some aloud. So
it must have been an evening of amazements for
Crane, in a borrowed suit of clothes. The one man
in America who had properly praised Tolstoy had
also praised him and he had heard a new sort of
verse, better than "The Charge of the Light Brigade"
and "The Burial of Moses" but he did not stop to let
his mind bask in all this; he walked over to the
Bowery and spent the rest of the night watching
drunken negroes play poker in the rear room of a
saloon.

Then he was suddenly absorbed in some kind of
research. He raided piles of old magazines in the
studio of Corwin Knapp Linson and complained to
the illustrator that nobody had written anything
worth reading about the Civil War. He dropped
in, one Sunday, at the house of Mrs. Armstrong—
once the Miss Brett who had spanked him for bury-
ing her nephew—and borrowed the *Century's*
"Battles and Leaders" after her father had assured
him that these were accurate. One afternoon he was
idle in the rooms of William Dallgren, watching
Dallgren sketch Acton Davies when Davies tossed
him Emile Zola's "Lâ Débâcle," in a translation.
Davies was a round youth who doted on Zola and
when Crane slung the book aside he was annoyed.

"I suppose you could have done it better?"

"Certainly," said Crane.

On April 2nd he sent back "Battles and Leaders of the Civil War" to Mrs. Armstrong with a note: "Thank you very much for letting me keep these so long. I have spent ten nights writing a story of the war on my own responsibility but I am not sure that my facts are real and the books won't tell me what I want to know so I must do it all over again, I guess." This is the birth notice of "The Red Badge of Courage."

His mind had gone swinging back to war in the recoil from failure in realities. "Maggie" was not absolute reporting. He had invented its small plot and only two incidents of the story were from the life —the fight in the saloon and the destruction of Maggie's lambrequin by her mother. But he was in full flight from the codes of naturalism. . . . Flight took him inevitably to his first passion. He had made games of battle when he was a child. He was always playing mentally and all the force of imagination dragged at him in his very genuine despair of methods to release the hiding vigour of his brain. He could stand through nights in a blizzard of late March to write "Men in the Storm" or sleep in a Bowery shelter to get at the truth of "An Experiment in Misery" but the emotions of a boy in battle he must find for himself, in himself, and the birth of the book was travail incomprehensible to men who have never hunted in themselves passions and the flood of acts to which they are alien. However, there had been a boy who went confidently off to make war on a world and a city. He had been beaten to shelter and had lurched up a lane in darkness on the arm of some stranger. He had been praised for his daring while his novel, like a retreating army, lay in unsold heaps and the maker of images was sure of his own clay. 20736

But "Maggie" was riding his neck. Howells saw no reason why the book should not be sold. "To this hour," he said in 1913, "I cannot understand the attitude of the dealers. I saw several of them personally and tried to interest Mr. Brentano. If Crane had cared to try that trick he might have disposed of 'Maggie' through certain stores which had the reputation of selling obscene paperbacks. I suppose that the profanity of his masterpiece would have appealed to High School boys. But he did not descend to the method and, on my suggestion, mailed copies to Dr. Parkhurst and another minister who were then interested in the condition of the slums. Neither acknowledged the gift and Crane told me, afterwards, that a Roman Catholic notable wrote that 'Maggie' was an insult to the Irish. I shall never understand what was found offensive in the little tragedy."

Howells might not understand but, as late as 1921, "Maggie" was described as "flippant and unfeeling" by a reviewer and it is plain that sardonic observance

of seduction, drunkenness and fatuous plebians
would not wash down the throats of booksellers in
1893.   The book came headlong against an American
mode in fiction.   These characters were poor and, so,
should have been treated more kindly.   Even in
the championship of Howells, one sees a slanting
attitude: the book was "a little tragedy" and the pity
of Maggie's case appears more sharply in his three
essays than any other feature of the story.   But he
was a champion and he shocked friends by his praise
of this grimness. . . . The Howells of 1893 had altered somewhat from the nervous friend who scolded
Mark Twain for writing "she combed me all to hell."
He had emerged from the warm fogs of Bostonian
eminence and was living among men whose theory
of things possible differed broadly from that of his
former group.   He had been lightly bidden to sit
still and talk while Saint Gaudens finished the model
of a quite naked woman who went on chewing gum
as though she were fully clad.   He was standing
beside Stanford White on the deck of a ferry when
some stoker fell from the stern of a tug and was
smashed by its screw to pulp that left on the waters
a lacquer of bloody oil.   The architect yelled, "Oh,
poor devil!" and then brought down both palms on
the rail of the ferry with another cry, "My God!
What colour!"   Thus, one sees in the realist's later
novels a weak and brief concession of the absolute:
a man might thrash another with a cowhide whip

and then vomit in repugnance: the good and kindly might in "New Leaf Mills," come off second best in a peculiar world; his ethical optimism sometimes waned into admission of things senseless, chill and real.

But neither Howells nor anybody else could sell "Maggie." Edward Marshall of the *Press* tried to persuade his paper to make a serial of it and in May 1893 Crane had some hope of a hundred dollars and a chance to hear what "Men of Sense" would think. There existed a collection of humans who were "men of sense" as differing from mere men. They were people not shocked by trifles who were willing to believe that he meant what he said. Marshall, not much older than himself, was a man of sense and Crane took heed when the young editor told him that his adjectives were often too heavy and that his coined adverbs were frequently difficult. So a sketch to be called "The Reluctant Voyagers," for which Corwin Linson made illustrations with Crane as a model, shows fewer adjectives, fewer adverbs and greater ease. But nobody bought it. Nor did anybody buy, immediately, "The Pace of Youth" which includes: "In the darkness stretched the vast purple expanse of the ocean, and the deep indigo sky above was peopled with yellow stars. Occasionally out upon the waters a whirling mass of froth suddenly flashed into view, like a great ghostly robe appearing, and then vanished, leaving the sea in its darkness, whence came those bass tones of the water's unknown emotion. . . . High in the sky soared an unassuming moon faintly silver." Not knowing that two eminent novelists of another land would at last honour his prose by adopting it, Crane had no consolation and no cash for "The Pace of Youth" in 1893.

In June he turned over three hundred copies of "Maggie" to Mrs. Armstrong for safekeeping: "Sometime or other somebody or other might buy some," and went to Edmund's house. He came downstairs often and read bits of his manuscript aloud to his brother. "The Red Badge of Courage" was being slowly examined and partly re-written. Edmund Crane could write pure English and his young brother made test of a clear intelligence. The man of business objected frequently, to sentences without verbs and to adjectives that had got loose from all mooring but he was excited by the battle, having himself started off to war at the age of seven.

Stephen Crane was not taking much advice. In September shooting had begun at Port Jervis and on the first of October he was feeling, "bully. Am going camping in Sullivan (County) with some other bobcats." In that company he spent three weeks but on some date of the month's last week he arrived in New York with a valise and a slight cold and the price of a pair of shoes in his pocket.

Having bought new shoes he used his last five cent

piece to descend on Edward Marshall in the office
of the *Press* through a cold rainstorm that soaked
his clothes. The two young men had a singular regard for each other. Marshall was a writer of some
skill and not a flattering reporter of New York. His
dismissal from the *Press* had been demanded more
than once by annoyed and powerful men and he had
not been dismissed, although no influence kept him
in place. When Crane passed beyond the point of
casual amity, his feeling became fixed and savage.
He liked Marshall and trusted him as simply as he
now asked for a job. Marshall sat on the corner
of a desk, swinging his watch chain around a finger
for a minute and then answered: "No. I'll take
all the special articles you can do, Stevie, but you are
made for better things. Don't waste your time."

Instead of asking for five dollars, Crane walked
out of the office and started uptown through the rain.
He tramped with two thirds of "The Red Badge of
Courage" in his valise from the tip of the city's
tongue to East Twenty Third Street and stumbled
into the rooms of Frederick Gordon in the Art Students' League building, a wildly fashioned barrack
"which squatted, slumbering and old, between two
exalted commercial structures which would have had
to bend afar down to perceive it. . . . The northward march of the city's progress had happened not
to overturn this aged structure, and it huddled there,
lost and forgotten, while the cloud-veering towers

strode on." Gordon, after a look at the shivering creature, got him out of his clothes and into bed. The artist's room was big enough for another cot and Crane stayed on after a week's violent illness. His cooking added infamy to his host's life and he placidly told an arriving Englishman, Holmes Bassett, that Mrs. Humphry Ward must be an idiot. Her celebrated novel, "Robert Elsmere" was a lot of higgling rubbish and so was most English writing.

Bassett had called on Gordon by mistake and was already embarrassed, talking to an utter stranger dressed in an undershirt who looked deplorably ill. This critical blast blew him from his feet and as he had met Mrs. Ward in London, he was shocked. So he went off to the Holland House and then came back, after ten days, to hunt up this irreverent character and take him to a prizefight at Madison Square Garden. Corbett was to give an exhibition and all the world was going. . . . The occasion became historic, suddenly. Crane dined at the Holland House with a man wearing a monocle and sat beside Bassett near the ringside while the smoky height of the great oval cavern filled with men. Presently Mark Twain appeared in a box with Robert Reid and the ruddy Stanford White. There rose a considerable stir. Clemens was in the papers, fighting ruin after the collapse of his printing scheme and a comber of sentiment splashed toward the tall figure, sheathed in furs, while the people of cheap

seats whistled, here and there, recognizing the clown
of innumerable lectures with his whitened hair and
the beauty of his beginning age. Crane sat staring
at "the divine amateur" in silence and on some question said, "I only like one of his books." Which
one? "Life on the Mississippi."

Corbett boxed. Clemens was led in state by Stanford White to the prizefighter's dressing room.
Crane went off to his borrowed bed and a christening
took place in a house near the Players' Club on
Gramercy Park. There was an Hungarian Band
playing. Mark Twain came at 10:45 and Richard
Harding Davis followed him. Walter Damrosch
made music on a piano while a tenor sang and people
began to discuss what names they would choose if
they could have the matter adjusted. Then Davis
wanted to know what name Clemens would have
liked had he been a woman? The humourist dal-
lied with the matter, then decided on "Petunia
Bloggs." The joke went around the room. Queerly,
Stanford White wanted to be called Evelina. Then
they began to christen famous people who were elsewhere. The Prince of Wales became "Lily" by al-
lusive process. Ellen Terry was suddenly "Roder-
ick Dhu"—it is not remembered why—and Davis
asked for a new name for Henry James.

"Oh," said Clemens, "call him Henrietta Maria."

This jape was in London six months later, but
Crane, a few blocks to the north of its making, was

far from well. He took more cold and Gordon had
to nurse him in the windy building of three entrances
where young fellows hunted each other with candles
by night to borrow twenty cents against the morning's breakfast. Bassett, no Bohemian, sometimes
took Crane out to dine and was pulled along the
Bowery, with his monocle. This glass delighted
Crane and he liked to play with its round when there
was nothing else for his fingers to caress. He must
have something to fondle or he wasn't comfortable.
Smoking seemed to mean just an object between his
fingers and a dead cigarette was quite as good as one
burning until he noticed the extinction and threw
the thing away. He hated champagne because it
made him dizzy after two glasses, but a white German wine rather pleased him, and meanwhile he told
Bassett all about bears, horses, dogs and sailing
boats. His opinions squirted out in shocking jets on
a conservative who was, at the time, devout. Marriage, Crane said, was a base trick on women, who
were hunted animals anyhow. A wedding was a
legal ceremony, if ceremony there must be, and of all
sects the Episcopal Church was the biggest inanity.
Men had been allowed to pervert the teachings of
Christ and Buddha into formulæ and there was no
such thing as sin "except in Sunday schools." Bassett went off to see an uncle in Ottawa with an impression of wild radicalism afoot on East Twenty
Third Street. But "Maggie" came to him by the

next mail inscribed: "This work is a mud-puddle, I am told on the best authority. Wade in and have a swim." So he learned that his acquaintance was a writer for the first time.

In February Crane took "The Red Badge of Courage" to a typist and left it for copy, finished and ready for anybody to read. Typewriting then was still expensive but thirty dollars seem heavy for the short book. Having paid fifteen of the fee, he got half the manuscript back and went up into Harlem to see Hamlin Garland. After one look, Garland lent another fifteen dollars and the whole treasury was out of pawn. On the twenty-fourth of February Crane wrote to Bassett: "I have just sold another book and my friends think it is pretty good and that some publisher ought to bring it out when it has been shown as a serial. It is a war-story and the syndicate people think that several papers could use it." He had sold "The Red Badge of Courage" to Irving Bacheller's young syndicate for less than a hundred dollars.

IV

FAME AND PREJUDICE

STEPHEN CRANE'S scarce letters are not often interesting. They have a formal running tone, now and then lifted by a phrase. Sometimes he exploded into an utterly informal and prolonged expression. These vital papers must have been dashed down at the end of a mood. They are seldom dated, seldom headed and recipients say that they were usually addressed haphazard. Thus, on some date of late November, 1894, and obviously from Port Jervis, comes: "If you hear that I have been hanged by the neck till dead on the highest hill of Orange County you may as well know that it was for killing a man who is really a pug—No, by the legs of Jehovah! I will not insult any dog by comparing this damned woman to it. There is a feminine mule up here who has roused all the bloodthirst in me and I don't know where it will end. She has no more brain than a pig and all she does is to sit in her kitchen and grunt. But every when she grunts something dies howling. It may be a girl's reputation or a political party or the Baptist Church but it

stops in its tracks and dies. Sunday I took a 13
yr. old child out driving in a buggy. Monday this
mule addresses me in front of the barber's and says,
'You was drivin' Frances out yesterday' and
grunted. At once all present knew that Frances and
I should be hanged on twin gallows for red sins. No
man is strong enough to attack this mummy because
she is a nice woman. She looks like a dried bean
and she has no sense, but she is a nice woman.
Right now she is aiming all her artillery at Cornelia's
new hat.[1] I have been deprived by heaven of any
knowledge of hats but it seems to be a very kindly
hat with some blue flowers on one side and a ribbon
on the other. But we rustle in terror because this
maggot goes to and fro grunting about it. If this
woman lived in Hester Street some son or brother of
a hat would go bulging up to her and say, 'Ah, wot
deh hell!' and she would have no teeth any more,
right there. She is just like those hunks of women
who squat on porches of hotels in summer and wher-
ever their eye lights there blood rises. Now, my
friend, there is a big joke in all this. This lady in
her righteousness is just the grave of a stale lust and
every boy in town knows it. She accepted ruin at
the hands of a farmer when we were all 10 or 11.
But she is a nice women and all her views of all
things belong on the tables of Moses. No man has
power to contradict her. We are all cowards any-

[1] Mrs. William Crane.

how. Bacheller thinks I had best start for Nevada as soon as possible, maybe before Christmas, but I should like to be with the family, of course."   Then, in a postscript, "Somebody has written clean from California about The Red Badge."

The story, cut into lengths convenient for the *Philadelphia Press* had surprised him by the number of letters that came showering through the Bacheller Syndicate.   Another surprise was less pleasing. Bacheller took him down to Philadelphia and the whole staff of the *Press* had swarmed up to congratulate him.   There were old soldiers among the printers and their words had been very warm.   Excitement or something more tangible gave him an attack of dyspepsia and this was new, painful and lasting.   He was used to colds, sore throats and chilblains but dyspepsia seemed unlawful, especially as it recurred.   In 1894, too, the heat of New York's summer had suddenly been "fog, like a Turkish bath's steam chamber, with the whole dressed city panting and scratching in its weight."   A trip to Scranton with Corwin Linson was a relief.   They reported and sketched the mining town for Bacheller with a prospect of another article on deep sea diving but the sea change did not come and Crane was much at Port Jervis in the later summer.   In Port Jervis he evolved a social theory that Elbert Hubbard bought for *The Philistine* together with an essay on charities in the New York Slums.   Hubbard lost these papers

on a train and Crane never replaced them but the
social theory remains, in a letter of Hubbard.

The world was full of old, plain and dull ladies
who sat about on porches and were omnipotent.
Nobody could argue with them; they ruled the universe; they blighted the scene. This bestial force
came from the education of all Americans by female
schoolteachers. Men were sent to school under the
power of dull, limited women and learned to cringe
from them. The habit was so stamped in males that
they never dared to argue with any woman and so
there should be more male teachers. The article on
the slums included some criticisms of Tolstoy, still
Crane's literary god although "The Kreutzer Sonata"
bored him so that he could not finish it—the thing
was "an old maid's picnic." He seems to have distrusted any novel favoured by elderly women,
clergymen or Frank R. Stockton, an author of the
time, harmless amusing and much petted by the
minor critics.

In 1894 he was enraged by Mrs. Frances Hodgson
Burnett's "Little Lord Fauntleroy" and encountering
two small boys who had been tricked out by their
mothers in imitation of Reginald Birch's too faithful
illustrations, in long curls and lace collars he coolly
gave the sufferers money to have their hair cut.
This act of altruism took place about September 1st
in the city of Albany and Crane carefully told his
alarmed hostess what he thought of "Lord Faunt-

leroy." His opinions of books never altered greatly. In 1899 he wrote: "No thanks. If the Whilomville stories seem like Little Lord Fauntleroy to you you are demented and I know that you are joking, besides. See here, my friend, no kid except a sick little girl would like Lord Fauntleroy unless to look at Birch's pictures for it. The pictures are all right."

This innocuous romance was printed in 1886 and its results sullied the lives of many small boys born in the decade following that date. Crane's rage was rooted in his dislike of sentimentalized children. Mrs. Burnett's shrewd bit of writing tells how one Cedric Errol, the grandson of an aged and gouty earl, reformed his ancestor and soothed the life of an English countryside. Crane had heard, somewhere, Matthew Arnold's "sweetness and light" and he tacked the phrase to "Little Lord Fauntleroy." As he seldom read books, an annoying novel left a scar in his mind, unhealed to his end. His impressions of Chicago, in January of 1895, were stained by a procession of Lord Fauntleroys met on a corner beside a church. That any young male should be draped in lace and velvet and made to wear long curls!

Bacheller was sending him west to write sketches with a free hand, as long as he finished the trip in Mexico, and Crane's course is hard to follow. Most of his letters have been lost and the sketches ap-

peared out of order.   He had, though, three immedi-
ate wishes.   He must see a cowboy ride.   He wanted
to be in a blizzard of the plains.   He must look at
the Mississippi because Elbert Hubbard had per-
suaded him to read "Huckleberry Finn" and 143
East Twenty Third Street had heard his grunt of
disgust over the lame conclusion of Mark Twain's
masterpiece.   Didn't the genius know any better?
A baby could have improved the end of "Huckleberry Finn"!   The boys stopped being boys and
were dolls.   So, as in the mind of Arnold Bennett,
"Life on the Mississippi" was always Twain's best
book.   It is not known that he saw much of the
Mississippi, but he had his two other wishes.   He
saw cowboys ride and visited a ranch near the border
of Nevada, where somebody gave him or sold him
some silver spurs.   He changed trains once at a
dreary junction town where was a hotel of a dreadful
blue that fascinated him.   His thirst for blues ran to
shades of cold electric tones and this blue was a
lugubrious, fainter tinge.   In a hotel painted so
loathsomely, some dire action must take place and,
after four years, he made it seem so.   But in Lincoln, Nebraska, on February 13th, he pushed himself
into an irony by trying to stop a fight in a drinking
place.   It appears that a very tall man was pound-
ing a rather small one and Crane shoved himself between them.   "But thus I offended a local custom.
These men fought each other every night.   Their

friends expected it and I was a darned nuisance with
my Eastern scruples and all that. So first everybody cursed me fully and then they took me off to a
judge who told me that I was an imbecile and let
me go; it was very saddening. Whenever I try to
do right, it don't."

A blizzard was raging at Lincoln but he found
warm weather in Little Rock, Arkansas, and hurried
off to look at Hot Springs. There he broke a tooth
on a dried persimmon's stone and saw five funerals.
"It rained funerals on me. I was soaked with lamentations and the hope of widows." New Orleans was
a pictorial disappointment, while Creole food gave
him more dyspepsia but when he reached San
Antonio, he fell in love with that maligned city and
with Texas. . . . All the adolescence in him frothed
to a head. His letters from San Antonio are almost
childish. A wonderful Greek cook broiled pompano.
Here was the monument to the defenders of the
Alamo with its legend: "Thermopylæ had its mes-
senger of defeat; the Alamo had none"; and that,
he wrote to Hilliard, boomed in his ears like the clash-
ing of war-bronze. Every night here was the blaze
of East Houston Street, in spring, with parading men
in real sombreros and the lace of veils flung across
Mexican eyes. Persons with parenthetic mous-
taches sat in saloons filled with antlers and lied about
old duels. A red-haired man swung his elbow
against Crane's arm to get a revolver from his belt

and aim it at an enemy, before the bartender threw a seidel and spoiled the show. He pulled a small girl out of the soapy little river that wriggles through the town and she told him for his trouble to go to hell.

One day he was lingering on the Alamo Plaza and distressed sounds hit his ear. He saw a sixteen-year-old boy, as tall as himself, sitting on the edge of the gutter, sobbing. Young Edward Grover had come southwest from Chicago to begin life freshly as a cowboy with a birthday gift of sixty dollars in his pocket. Now the pocket was empty and the officers of Fort Sam Houston would not let him become a recruit. Crane marched this wretch into a restaurant, fed him thoroughly and took him straight to the railroad station. At Saint Louis, the homegoing runaway met an uncle who could telegraph back funds to Crane. Six days later, Grover had a note:

Dear Deadeye Dick:
Thanks for sending back my money so fast. The hotel trun me out, as my friends of the Bowery say and I was living in the Mex diggings with a push of sheep men till my boss in New York wired me money.

Now, old man, take some advice from a tough jay from back East. You say your family is all right and nobody bothers you. Well, it struck me that you are too young a kid[1] and too handsome to be free and easy around where

[1] Crane used the word long before it was popular in fiction.

a lot of bad boys and girls will take your pennies. So better stay home and grow a mustache before you rush out into the red universe any more.

Yours sincerely,
STEPHEN CRANE

In that Mexican lodging house he met a blushless rogue who, peddling illicit drink to the thirsty soldiery of Leon Springs in 1917, called himself Keenan. This man had charms; he was a Bowery boy who had wandered away from police and friends. He told Crane a tale of shooting down some Mexicans who tried to drive his sheep from a waterhole. The slaughter was a simple gesture of carelessness for at once he sold his sheep to them and retired from the pass. Crane sent him, in 1897, a copy of the *Century Magazine* with "A Man and Some Others" and Keenan hated Crane ever after for spoiling the point of the story.

The enchantment of Texas was partly equine. He rode a mule in the Painted Desert of Arizona but again, in Mexico, there were all sorts of horses and a little bay that carried him through a real adventure faithfully reported in "Horses—One Dash." . . . Crane and a Mexican guide, Miguel Itorbide, were benighted in a village suddenly invaded by a fashionable bandit, Ramon Colorado, and his followers. Diaz, the president-dictator of Mexico did not discourage a certain easy freedom in rural administration and small groups of banditry went cheerfully about their business within a hundred miles of the capital. Colorado heard that an American was lodged in the village and determined to absorb any money or luxuries that Crane might have with him—Then, exactly as in the story, a train of peripatetic harlots arrived on their way to some rejoicing in Mexico City and Colorado went to inspect. Crane and his guide crept from the hut and raced across the plain on their horses with Colorado's gang half a mile behind them. The pale uniforms of the rurales, the mounted constabulary of the district, came to solve the difficulty and a lieutenant sat cursing Colorado while the bandit tried to apologize for having annoyed a friend of the government. This business was delicious to Crane. . . . He had watched terrific brawls while, dressed in his worst clothes, he sat in Bowery dives and lodging houses, but he had never been so closely threatened and the detail of his emotions pumps through "Horses—One Dash" in a clear ripple of self-examination, sardonic always.

Let it be stated that the mistress of this boy's mind was fear. His search in æsthetic was governed by terror as that of tamer men is governed by the desire of women. "Maggie" had represented the terror of an environment tinged by social judgment. In all the Mexican and Texan sketches appears, as in "The Red Badge of Courage," a vision of man's identity faced by its end, by incomprehensible death. One gets the solid courage of the marshal of Yellow Sky who shoves annihilation from him by a simple statement; the rogue of "A Man and Some Others" dies easily because he is bound by contract to defend his flock. In the true story, "Horses" and the fanciful "Five White Mice," one sees Crane himself, recording his own pulse before a shadow which he refused to kneel and worship. He could be afraid, and afraid with all the quivering imagination of an artist—here stood the great death and here, mentally or in flesh, stood he. But his recording of the state is never more than civilly sympathetic. The boy of "Five White Mice" stands with a drunkard on each hand and the cloudy group of Mexicans before him, speculating on his friend's attitude after the slaughter. "The other Kid would mourn his death. He would be preternaturally correct for some weeks, and recite the tale without swearing. But it would not bore him. For the sake of his dead comrade he would be glad to be preternaturally correct and to recite the tale without swearing." Then the tortured thought veers off to a memory of a summer hayfield and to the wonder of a distant crooning stream. And then he steps forward and the great death steps back. The Mexicans retire up the dim street. Nothing has happened. The emotion has projected its intensity against nonsense, against a posture of some loungers. It is the last point in futility, the hurtle of mighty chords on an unhearing ear. . . . That this work was outside the mood of his time and his nation everybody knows.

Notoriety now jumped on him while he tramped the streets of Mexico City with his waistcoat pockets filled with opals given him by Charles Gardner, an American engineer, invalid after smallpox in the brilliant, lazy town where Crane saw, for the first time, the Latin consent to public pleasures. "You can sit at a table in front of a Café—a real café—and drink cool drinks. Nobody comes up and says, Stop! The Yankees and the Englishmen get drunk sometimes and make noises at the circus but the Mexicans make noises just at the bullfights." The bullfights were disgusting to him because horses were killed there, an unthinkable sacrilege. Mr. Gardner, reading the *New York Herald* saw that an absurd book of poems had appeared and asked across a table, "Is this poet Stephen Crane related to you?"

"I'm him," said Crane.

A fog rests on the birth of "Black Riders," sold to Copeland and Day of Boston in 1894. Crane was careless about dates. His own judgment, "I wrote the things in February of 1893" cannot be true because he had not then dined with William Dean Howells and had not heard the critic read Emily Dickinson's verses aloud. The testimony of Hamlin Garland and John Northern Hilliard must be correct and the startling lines were written sometime after the first of April 1893. Some of them were read by John Barry at a public meeting of literary persons in March of 1894, without applause. They came into Crane's head, while he was depressed one night and it seemed, almost, that somebody dictated them to him. The whole manuscript was twice lost, once by Crane himself in an elevated railway car and once by a friend who left the shabby papers somewhere and had to ransack New York for them. They existed in the autumn of 1894 as proof sheets which Frederick Gordon had in his pocket while he helped Crane gather facts in the crowds watching bulletins of the mayoral election which temporarily took New York's affairs from the orderly pillage of Tammany Hall into the sloppy ineffectiveness of the Reform party's hands. Copeland and Day issued "Black Riders" with a clever design by Gordon for the cover of the handsome little book which came out in April of 1895 and, with two favourable reviews in objection, the reading nation was told at once that Stephen Crane was mad.

The nation had been offered unrhymed sonnets of Anna Brackett and that Walt Whitman wrote long poems without rhymes was an established fact. The English even liked Whitman's concoctions. But "Black Riders and Other Lines" was the work of some pert maniac and opinions to the contrary in *The Bookman* and *The Lotos* had no weight. Here was simple insanity finely printed:

"Charity, thou art a lie,
A toy of women,
A pleasure of certain men.
In the presence of justice,
Lo, the walls of the temple
Are visible
Through thy form of sudden shadows."

That was rude and pretty bad. Worse came:

"I saw a man pursuing the horizon;
Round and round they sped.
I was disturbed at this:
I accosted the man.
'It is futile,' I said,
'You can never—'
'You lie,' he cried,
And ran on."

"Two or three angels
Came near to the earth.
They saw a fat church.
Little streams of black people
Came and went continually.
And the angels were puzzled
To know why the people went thus,
And why they stayed so long within."

"If I should cast off this tattered coat,
And go free into the mighty sky;
If I should find nothing there

But a vast blue,
Echoless, ignorant,—
What then?"

"God lay dead in heaven;
Angels sang the hymn of the end;
Purple winds went moaning,
Their wings drip-dripping
With blood
That fell upon the earth.
It, groaning thing,
Turned black and sank.
Then from the far caverns
Of dead sins
Came monsters livid with desire.
They fought,
Wrangled over the world,
A morsel.
But of all the sadness this was sad,—
A woman's arms tried to shield
The head of a sleeping man
From the jaws of the final beast."

In the Bowery he had seen a young streetwalker
cover the head of a drunken procurer with her body
while the fellow's assailants were trying to stamp his
face to pieces. Crane ran to bring help and the police arrested the girl for cursing. The exact mor-
ality of the Irish police amused Crane considerably.)

"A man feared that he might find an assassin;
Another that he might find a victim.

One was more wise than the other."

. .   .   .

"I walked in a desert.
And I cried,
'Ah, God, take me from this place!'
A voice said, 'It is no desert.'
I cried, 'Well, but—
'The sand, the heat, the vacant horizon.'
A voice said, 'It is no desert.' "

A man's perception of beauty in disastrous circumstances should have been phrased with more prolix
sentiment in 1895.   But Richard Watson Gilder and
others found pleasure in:

  , "Places among the stars,
Soft gardens near the sun,
Keep your distant beauty;
Shed no beam upon my weak heart.
Since she is here
In a place of blackness,
Not your golden days
Nor your silver nights
Can call me to you.
Since she is here
In a place of blackness,
Here I stay and wait."

But the vision of the world as a rudderless ship
"going ridiculous voyages, making quaint progress,
turning as with serious purpose before stupid winds,"
had no claim on a public which was reading Fitz-

gerald's quatrains just then with a delighted sense
of ethical exploration. Omar Khayyám might suit
the awakened hedonism of a nation still taught to
recite the stuff of Longfellow but "Black Riders"
suited nobody. The poems were bombast and drivel
and obscene and that was completely all there was
to the matter. But Crane was now somebody and
he had expected this blast before he dedicated the
book to Hamlin Garland. His friends, with some
exceptions in the shapes of Hilliard, Gordon, Linson
and Hubbard, had openly told him he was an affected ass, So, arriving in New York in May, he
took condolences serenely and said, "Some of the pills
are pretty darñed dumb, anyhow. But I meant
what I said," and being asked if he admired Stéphane
Mallarmé answered, "I don't know much about Irish
authors."

He was made welcome at the new Lantern Club of
journalists and editors in a crazy added story on the
roof of an old building near Brooklyn Bridge. Irving Bacheller, Thomas Masson, Edward Marshall,
Willis Hawkins, Richard Gilder, John Langdon
Heaton—whose wife was "the most sensible woman
in New York" to Crane—and some others lunched
there almost daily. Crane shook hands with Richard Harding Davis for the first time, gave the best
choice of his Mexican opals to Corwin Linson, then
let the others vanish among "the Wild Indians" of
the Art Students' League Building, save one kept

carefully for his niece, Helen, his brother William's daughter, who lost it later at school in Switzerland. Then he went up with his silver spurs and some woven blankets to Hartwood, a hamlet of Sullivan County, easily reached from Port Jervis. There Edmund Crane had taken charge of some undeveloped property and had a simple house where Crane lay grinning over the reviews of "Black Riders" and taught his nieces to play fan-tan.

Ripley Hitchcock bought "The Red Badge of Courage" for Appleton's in December of 1894 but Crane's trip to Mexico had delayed correction of the proofs and the book did not appear until October 3rd, 1895. Hitchcock was a man of extraordinary shrewdness. He could see the merits of "The Red Badge of Courage" and of such transient dullness as the forgotten "David Harum" with equal speed. He nicely predicted the success of "The Red Badge" in August of 1895 and saw the prediction come off by the first of January. The success has become a legend in American publishing. It is still commonly stated that the book did not sell until the English reviews in January lifted it to notice. The facts, as taken from amalgamated statements are these: All or nearly all the American reviews were enthusiastic and booksellers in New York bought large numbers of copies. But from Crane's hand on December 24th, 1895: "Mr. Hitchcock tells me that the book does not sell much in New York. It has gone to about 4500, though, and many of them have been sent west." At one bookshop, Leggett's, only two copies had been sold by the tenth of January. . . . Then, in middle January, the city began to buy "The Red Badge of Courage" and the sale mounted so swiftly that Edgar Saltus, who in October wrote that Crane had outdone Zola, Tolstoy and Kipling in a breath was now, on February 6th, moved to write to Charles Devlin: "A man sometimes yearns for the power to write vulgar inanity and sell it by the cart-load to fools. I hear that Stephen Crane has made twenty thousand dollars out of his trash." Devlin called the exquisite's attention to his former praise of the book and their interesting correspondence untimely ceased.

The history of a triumph is always dull. The unfavourable reaction to Crane's masterpiece is better worth study. Copies of "The Red Badge" were returned to Brentano's store in New York because the book held no "love-story" and it was sometimes returned because it was too grim. Two specimens of the first issue are scattered with bitter notes in the tremulous handwriting of some veteran who wrote: "Insulting," "unpatriotic," "damned nonsense" abreast of each sentence describing the young soldiers' fears in the blank wildness of his flight from the first day's battle. A clergyman in Illinois, George Stephen Crane who had served in a regiment at Chancellorsville was assailed by letters from old

friends either praising his memory or damning him
for betraying confidences made at that less sentimental moment when his comrades were in retreat
from the Southern army. Crane, himself, had letters profoundly pointing out that the boy's return to
camp with his damaged head and his acceptance of
his friend's belief that the bloodstains come from a
wound taken in battle make up a nasty comment on
the hero. Irony, says Carl Van Vechten, should
always be carefully underlined in an American
novel. And there is no notice, save that of William
Dean Howells, printed in 1895 which mentions the
ironies chasing themselves through "The Red
Badge." That critics of the day should note: "Mr.
Crane's interesting novel contains no strictures on
the cruel uselessness of war": was to be expected.
Merely to expose is never enough for the prim intelligences posted as guides to the American public.
Then, as now, their vision of the artist in letters is
the cloudy image of a poet in solemn posture on some
sanitary stage, dealing out commonplace evidence
of man's imperfection and urging on the universal
good.

The comedic element of "The Red Badge" probably had little notice at the time. But, very soon,
certain episodes were imitated. Within a year the
business of the lad who turns over his letter of fare-
well to Henry before the battle appeared in adap-
tation twice. The quarrels of the two boys could

be fitted into other scenes and were, promptly. . . . The biographer has been reproached for pointing out, elsewhere, that Alan Seeger's graceful poem, still current, with its line: "I have a rendezvous with death": was suggested by the tenth chapter of Crane's novel but Seeger's admiration of the book was known to his friends. The flowery advance of the banners has been precisely imitated in English and American war tales to the number of three hundred and ten times. The finish of the tenth chapter, the finding of the dead man in the wood, the row between the regiment's commander and the disgusted general and the description of the fires by night have been used ceaselessly. Crane's effect on Anglo-American prose has never been questioned by critics of any competence and his clear departure from the traditions of written English startled his day. There were vigorous catcalls and brayings, of course. It was passionately urged that no decent youth should describe emotions in terms of colours, that his grammar was wildly moulded to the needs of a point. But he was indisputably famous at the age of twenty-four, by reason of a book written, or designed, before his twenty-second birthday.

The act fell on academic culture as noisily as though a broken drumstick smote a plane of limp velvet. Crane had letters of praise from Bliss Perry, William Graham Sumner and Brander Matthews but recognition of living art had no place in the universities of the decade and Barrett Wendell, pausing in the consideration of Restoration comedy at Harvard, told one of his students that the book was sensational trash, then resumed his sour brilliance. So far as penetrable, smart society knew nothing of any such novel, for the Englishman already quoted in this history's second chapter vainly hunted in 1897 for somebody of New York's grandiose flock to make him known to Crane and at a dinner of forty found only one couple,—the late Frederick Whitridge and his wife—who had ever heard of the author. But Boston rolled in its shrines and the new writer was asked swiftly to appear. He was pointed out to visitors at a football game in Cambridge, in latter November, and stood shyly for a few minutes in the famous drawing room of Mrs. Fields.

Elbert Hubbard gave a dinner for him on December 19th in Buffalo and Crane stammered out something which, in the memory of Claude Bragdon, the dinner's master of ceremonies, was hardly a speech. Some of the guests took the party as an elaborate joke on Crane who must be rather mad or a posturer but excitement was growing in the vague kingdom of arts and the blaze of the English reviews lighted up January. Harold Frederic's letter to the *New York Times* was carefully arranged so that Henry James might know how little Frederic thought of his judgments—James having recommended Heinemann's new publication in Frederic's presence—but this war of two expatriates had no meaning in America and Crane was pleased by a note from Frederic while he rode his new horse, Peanuts, about Hartwood. The magazines were suddenly on his track and to *McClure's* went the whole collection of Texan and Mexican stories. Meanwhile Ripley Hitchcock was urging that "Maggie" be altered and published and Crane's old friend, Harry Thompson, wanted "George's Mother" for Edward Arnold as soon as it should be finished. The crowd at the Lantern Club wanted him to write a tale with a newspaperman as hero, of course, and people came driving compliments at him from every quarter. One of these was Richard Harding Davis, who did not particularly like Crane but who chose to make himself an agent of the younger man's reputation. The air was full of projects: he should write a political novel: he should write a play with Clyde Fitch. "It seems that I can do any damn thing I want to but be let alone," he wrote in February but walking with a friend up Broadway, elation swelled. It was pleasant to stroll to dinner at Mouquin's and to be a success.

2

Weir Mitchell was a practising, experienced neurologist as well as a narrator of modest historical tales. He once put on paper a speculation:

"The phenomena of envy are very much more marked among artists than in other professions. Invariably or nearly so, these take the form of gossiping stories about the personal character of a successful writer and the stories always show the same trend: the successful man is given to heavy indulgence in alcohol or to irregular use of drugs. The point is most interesting when one considers that artists are perpetually demanding for themselves the license of conduct which they deplore in print." These two methods of subterranean attack were in full use against Crane before March of 1896.

He had a trick of using small formulas in conversation and, now, when he was pressed to write some story which seemed too dull or too fantastic he began to say, "Oh, I'd have to get too drunk to write that." That this was hardly circumspect is plain and part of Crane's legend became fixed: he was obliged to get drunk before he could write at all. This had no currency among his friends but it was probably gospel in the bars of Mouquin's restaurant and of Louis Martin's café. The fiction of a successful man aided in his success by alcohol is very flattering to the less successful.

Here appears the shape of a forgotten and vanished being whose name was Thomas McCumber. He was very tall, very handsome and usually very tipsy in the popular bars between the years 1895 and 1904 when he died in a hospital of paresis.

His card bore the word "Photographer" in one corner and he once lived at the old Gilsey House for some months of 1896. He also once lived at a boarding house in East 19th Street where James Huneker knew him casually as a clever talker. It is faintly recalled that Crane had a nodding acquaintance with this man and did not seem to like him. He was described by O. Henry as "an infernal nuisance" but he was genial and he talked, apparently, in an amusing fashion. On a definite date, then, February 22nd, 1896, he made himself responsible for the statement that Crane took morphine.

In March of 1896 Crane seems to have been conscious that he was under fire. His last note to Wallis McHarg, dated from Hartwood, says: "When people see a banker taking a glass of beer in a café, they say, There is Smith. When they behold a writer taking a glass of beer, they say, Send for the police! No great law of nature can be proved from this but it pretty often hits me that people are ingenious blockheads. I have been to Washington about a book on political society for Mr. McClure but I came straight back." His further letters to McHarg are lost but in another he mentioned that some lying story had upset his friends and that a man hardly known to him was to blame.

The rumour of morphine had already reached Ripley Hitchcock and he diplomatically asked Crane's

views on the taking of drugs. Crane did not approve. His liberalism had certain inset features.
The ordinary prejudices of formal codes simply
washed down from his mind but drug-taking was
a habit of fools and he had seen the dreary end of
it on the East Side. A man of sense would not take
drugs and, two years later, he repeated the opinion
to James Huneker.

"As soon," said Harding Davis, "as Mr. Crane's
success began there were ugly stories set in circula-
tion about his private life. When he died his friends
found it necessary to issue a denial that he took
drugs. The yarn was absurd on its very face but it
was told constantly. . . . I was never intimate with
Crane but his best friends assured me that the story
was false and they were not men to lie. He had a
decided prejudice against drugtaking which I heard
him express frequently at dinners and at the Lan-
thorn Club. But appearances were against him. He
smoked constantly and he was very sallow and very
thin. To see him through the smoke of a restaurant and to be told that he ate morphine would not
have surprised me. But I know a great deal about
the signs of the drug habit and Mr. Crane had none
of them. Neither did it seem to me that he drank
excessively. I remember that he disliked champagne, for instance, and as far as my memory serves
me, he mostly stuck to dark beer. I know nothing
about his relations with women and the story told

about him in connection with some actress or artist's model was untrue to my knowledge."

The story yields up these facts. Crane was sitting with Acton Davies and Clyde Fitch in Mouquin's restaurant one night near the first of 1896 and a woman of some notoriety came up to ask Crane for a loan. This person had a number of titles and was sometimes married, informally or formally, but her actual name seems to have been Doris Watts. Crane had met her in 1895 as the titular wife of an acquaintance and she now appealed to him for a loan of fifty dollars. So he borrowed a blank check from Clyde Fitch and gave an amount not known. Acton Davies warned him that he would never be repaid. Crane's own statement of the sequel was dictated in November of 1899 and was also made verbally to two friends. The woman, then known as Mrs. Bowen, began to worry him with letters asking for more funds on the plea that she was destitute and wanted to "reform." . . . He had a recklessly generous attitude toward women of all sorts and perhaps he was touched. He seems to have sent her several small checks which came to a total of $150 or thereabouts. But she wrote to him incessantly and at last threatened to come to Hartwood. This was a light variety of blackmail, of course, and Crane came to New York to have done with it. She was not sufficiently destitute to have dismissed her maid, a negress, who let Crane into her rooms on West 48th Street. "I leaned on the door and told her to drop this nonsense. There was one of those horrors called Turkish corners in the room with a shield stuck full of knives. She lost her temper and grabbed a knife from the shield. It flew over my shoulder and stuck into the wood beside my ear and quivered so that I can still hear the noise." The disconsolate heroine then swooned, by rote, into the arms of her maid and Crane went away, hatless. He borrowed a cap from a friend whose studio was in 30th Street and retired to Hartwood.

The story was abroad by July and its general form was that Crane had seduced and then abandoned some girl of respectable parentage. The story naturally varied: she was a trusting artist's model: a country girl: a virgin actress. In July, Willis Clarke, a young fellow who was trying fiction, asked his brother starting for New York, to make inquiries about Stephen Crane. In the old Cairo restaurant, Clarke's brother was told that Crane was notoriously the father of a child by an unhappy girl who now was loose on the town. The Cairo was an excellent springboard for such information, as, with the exception of the Haymarket on Sixth Avenue, it was probably the rowdiest large night resort in New York at the time.

However, Crane was fair game for any legend. Hadn't he published a book of affected poems, one

of which denied a Commandment? *Appleton's* had
issued the slightly revised "Maggie" in June and it
was plainly a shocking work although the reviews
were civil. Besides, reporting for the *Press* the
opening of a music hall called the Broadway Gardens, he had already been published as the hero of
a fight with a policeman who had bullied a girl
about her business in the rear of the hall. . . . Crane
was boyishly proud of the incident and discussed it
with his brothers. He made a vehement attempt to
destroy the policeman totally and was locked up all
night but dismissed by some sensible judge in the
morning. . . . A distinct flavour of "Maggie" mingled in the gossip and some of his admirers were
seriously told that in order to write of her fate, he
had seduced a Bowery beauty and then thrown her
to the wolves. All this compounded silliness was
stirring and, in August, the drowning core of the
fable herself appeared in the offices of a young attorney with four letters from Crane as evidence that
he owed her support. But all the letters began and
ended formally and the checks were described as
"loans." The attorney refused the case. She then
attempted to have a warrant issued for Crane's arrest but was denied. A paragraph on August 23rd
reports: "A young woman well known to habitués
of the gayer restaurants along Broadway yesterday
applied for a bench warrant to right the 'wrongs'
done her by a prominent young writer of sensational

fiction. The application was denied as her evidence did not seem sufficient and the lady left the court room on the arm of a gentleman whose buttonhole of lilies of the valley had already interested onlookers."

It is impossible, now, to retrace the jigging route of this scandal. It blew here and there fragrantly and entered the offices of *The Century* where lay the manuscript of "A Man and Some Others" sold to the magazine by Paul Reynolds. In early autumn the literary agent was hastily sent for by the editor who demanded: "What does Crane mean by getting into such a mess when he's sold a story to *us?*"

The world of journals, though, had no space for the spite of a pretty drab against an eccentric author. Front pages must be cleared for the whirling news of a great duel between two voices—the barytone roar of William Jennings Bryan and the milder basso of William McKinley. It was now understood that some numerical incantation known as the silver standard would either make everybody sixteen times richer or would ruin the United States. Few minds were strong enough to comprehend the reasoning of this process but a plain case of the people against the wicked rich had been made out and as Mr. Bryan had already chosen the rôle of buffoon in the arid comedy of American religion he had the support of countless women in the midland where they have always been quietly powerful in our politics, so the Nebraskan was shown in posters as a mailed knight spearing the fat dragon of plutocracy and Democratic bankers were secretly heaving funds into the hands of Mark Hanna, the fat dragon's visible jockey.   It was the battle of a noise against a timid, dully honourable man in hidden armour but the nation shook in genuine hysteria until election day when Ohio contributed another of her characteristic sons to the presidential gallery and Hanna, worn out by exertion, lighted his cigars in capitalistic peace. . . . Crane was shooting along the coloured hills with his brother and the charming setter, Chester, and stopping to ask, "Will, isn't that cloud green? . . . But they wouldn't believe it if I put it in a book."

V

FILIBUSTERING

H E loved babies, horses, oceans or anything
that offered an enigmatic surface to his
thought. This comes strongly to view in a
letter of 1895, when he was reading the criticism of
Henry James: "What, though, does the man mean
by disinterested contemplation? It won't wash. If
you care enough about a thing to study it, you are
interested and have stopped being disinterested.
That's so, is it not? Well, Q.E.D. It clamours in
my skull that there is no such thing as disinterested
contemplation except that empty as a beerpail look
that a babe turns on you and shrivels you to grass
with. Does anybody know how a child thinks?
The horrible thing about a kid is that it makes no
excuses, none at all. They are much like breakers
on a beach. They do something and that is all there
is in it." So he put them under a detached observation and played with them by the hour. The detachment was so perfect that his tales of childhood
in the town of Whilomville were called cruel when
they appeared. But he had an absolute sentiment

for children and on November 12, 1896, he wrote to
a Miss Catherine Harris: "Thank you very much
for your letter on Maggie. I will try to answer your
questions properly and politely. Mrs. Howells was
right in telling you that I have spent a great deal
of time on the East Side and that I have no opinion
of missions. That—to you—may not be a valid answer since perhaps you have been informed that I
am not very friendly to Christianity as seen around
town. I do not think that much can be done with
the Bowery as long as the . . . (blurred) . . . are
in their present state of conceit. A person who
thinks himself superior to the rest of us because he
has no job and no pride and no clean clothes is
as badly conceited as Lillian Russell.[1]   In a story of
mine called 'An Experiment in Misery' I tried to
make plain that the root of Bowery life is a sort
of cowardice. Perhaps I mean a lack of ambition or
to willingly be knocked flat and accept the licking.
The missions for children are another thing and if
you will have Mr. Rockefeller give me a hundred
street cars and some money I will load all the babes
off to some pink world where cows can lick their
noses and they will never see their families any
more. My good friend Edward Townsend—have
you read his 'Daughter of the Tenements'?—has
another opinion of the Bowery and it is certain to
be better than mine. I had no other purpose in

[1] Crane singularly disliked this actress for reasons unknown.

writing 'Maggie' than to show people to people as they seem to me.[1] If that be evil, make the most of it."

Then, on November 29th, writing from Jacksonville, Florida, to his brother William a horse rises in the directions for his will and precedes the appointment of his literary executors—Howells, Garland, Willis Hawkins and Ripley Hitchcock. William Crane was to be his sole executor and to receive a third of the estate, Edmund Crane was to have another third and the remainder was divided between his two other brothers. But the horse, Peanuts: ". . . my saddle horse I would not like to have sold. I would prefer that he be kept in easy service at Hartwood and have him cared for as much as possible by Ed himself or by somebody whom it is absolutely certain would not maltreat him . . . and all I can add now is my love to you and Cornelia and all the babies."

Filibustering was much the fashion in the years 1895 and 1896. The condition of Cuba was now so acutely revolutionary that European papers were wondering why the Cleveland administration didn't interfere, just as in two years they would be indignant that the McKinley administration had interfered. A century of inartistic government tinted

[1] "You abuse me for objectivity, calling it indifference to good and evil. . . . It's my task simply to show people as they are." Anton Tchehov.

with sadism had wearied Cuba. Thirty thousand
men were admittedly in revolt and thousands more
were under suspicion. Enterprising ships passed
carefully from the ragged coast of Florida, laden
with cartridges and guns, to meet signals of the insurrectionists flashed from the rim of the tormented
island. The Bacheller Syndicate had sent Crane in
a hurry southward with a belt full of gold and his
ambition was to see real war. He also took along
for revision the manuscript of "The Third Violet"
which tells how a young impressionist painter wooed
a wealthy beauty, in dire fear of her all the while,
and won her in a drawing room where a colossal
chandelier cast malign lights, as if a piece of prose
could fulfil a buried wish of his twentieth year.
But Jacksonville bored him, on first view, and he
was alone who liked to have people always around
him: "The town looks like soiled pasteboard that
some lunatic babies have been playing with. The
same old women are sitting on the hotel porches
saying how well the climate suits them and hurling
the same lances with their eyes to begin bloodshed. . . . I went down the shore some distance
yesterday and watched the combers come counting in.
Sometimes their addition changes to multiplication
and the music is confounded, like a war of drummerboys." He had thrown a dinner party into gay
convulsions lately by insisting that music was, "Addition without pain" but the mathematical basis of

music was not much discussed in 1896 and Crane could not quote Leibnitz in support of his view as he had never heard of Leibnitz but the remark stuck in the memory of James Huneker who thereafter insisted that Crane was an intuitive natural philosopher. Meanwhile the "war of drummerboys" did not console him for the absence of friends and he desperately tried to finish "Peace and War," as he called it. But Tolstoy's endless panorama annoyed him. "He could have done the whole business in one third of the time and made it just as wonderful. It goes on and on like Texas."

Complete darkness covers him, then, until December 29th when the small and elderly steamer *Commodore* dropped down the river from Jacksonville commanded by a strapping young Irish shipmaster, Edward Murphy, and containing besides cased guns and a ton of cartridges, a large party of Cuban insurrectionists headed by one Delgado. Crane's instinctive aversion to sheer theatrical points would not let him believe that a plot had been arranged to frustrate the cruise of the *Commodore* but threats were shouted at her crew in Spanish while she lay at the pier taking on coal and a Cuban student, Juan Broch, on his way northward, heard two men saying, "It is all fixed. She will sink" in Castilian while he lingered on the dock after bidding good-bye to a friend. Jacksonville was a nest of Cuban interests. Ralph D. Paine reports in "Roads of Adventure" the location of the Cuban patriotic committee and the Spanish secret service may well have been busy with the *Commodore*. The Spanish diplomatic powers at Washington had been protesting all autumn against the open sailing of filibustering ships from American ports. In a general embarrassment, the United States navy patrolled the coast and Spanish gunboats were watchful. The *Commodore* went downstream and met a squall as she passed from the St. John's River into pure salt-water. Crane thought the ship no more seaworthy than an ice house although she had been lately examined for re-insurance and that she should begin to fill abreast of St. Augustine was not strange but his last impression of the engine room stayed deeply in his mind, with the fixity of all scenes in which the red he so loved was the commanding tone: "Water was swirling to and fro with the roll of the ship, fuming greasily around the half strangled machinery that still attempted to perform its duty. Steam arose from the water, and through its clouds shone the red glare of the dying fires. As for the stokers, death might have been with silence in this room. . . ."

The seasick Cubans lost their heads even before Captain Murphy turned the *Commodore* toward the shore. Their leader, Delgado, lost his temper and the jarring noise of quarrels rubbed on Crane's nerves. No one had slept for a day and a night and

Crane was already ill before the ship began to founder. He watched her as she "shifted and settled as calmly as an animal curls down in the bushgrass" while he crouched beside the injured captain in a ten foot dinghy, the last of the three boats to leave the heeling side of the steamer that disappeared noiselessly. "She might," he said, "have blown up to celebrate the New Year but she did not. She calmly left us orphans." The orphans were Captain Murphy, the ship's cook, Montgomery, an oiler, William Higgins and Crane. Now, none of them knew the colour of the sky.

"The Open Boat" is Crane's report of this wandering and Ralph Paine's statement shows that the sketch was corrected by Captain Murphy's memory. They rowed and the wind helped them toward their general aim, the point of Mosquito Inlet with its lighthouse and station. Murphy was helpless against the water jar in the stern and Crane changed places with the oiler, Higgins, constantly. . . . They talked of food. "Canton flannel gulls flew near and far. Sometimes they sat down on the sea, near patches of brown seaweed that rolled over the waves with a movement like carpets on a line in a gale. The birds sat comfortably in groups and were envied by some in the dinghy. . . . One came and evidently decided to alight on the top of the captain's head." Incorrigible, Crane's humour forbade him to neglect the absurd sight of Murphy timidly

waving a hand to keep this gull from his soaked
hair. Crests tumbled spray into the boat and the
point of the lighthouse danced to view when the
dinghy rose on the "jagged" waves. . . . A work of
art progressed while his back ached with the work
of the oar. Then followed woe; they were seen
from the beach; men waved—then night came without rescue and a shark circled the drifting boat with
a luminous wake. . . . "When it occurs to a man
that nature does not regard him as important . . .
he at first wishes to throw bricks at the temple and
he hates deeply the fact that there are not bricks
and no temples. Any visible expression of nature
would surely be pelleted with his jeers. Then, if
there be no tangible thing to hoot, he feels, perhaps, the desire to confront a personification and
indulge in pleas, . . . saying, 'Yes, but I love myself.' " . . . Dawn came and they turned the dinghy
to the bobbing shore knowing they must swim after
its inevitable upset. So they swam in a gripping
current and Crane was flung clear across the floating
boat by a comber. But even in that iced, stupen-
dous motion he must see the water flask bouncing
gaily while he thrashed. They got ashore, somehow and a wave smashed the spine of the oiler,
Higgins, so that "a still and dripping shape was
carried slowly up the beach and the land's welcome
for it could be only the different and sinister hospitality of the grave."

He was not well, suffering from some intestinal trouble, when the *Commodore* sailed and now he had spent fifty hours almost sleepless, drenched with water, imperfectly fed on diluted whiskey and biscuit. It is the opinion of his brother that health never returned and he certainly did himself no good by tramping and riding through the swamps below Jacksonville for weeks after the disaster. Rumours of very secret small expeditions kept the town wakeful and the Navy was now most active off shore, sweeping plumes of searchlight across the skies at night. The tug *Three Friends* was the villain of the Spanish Government, now, and Crane might yearn for Cuba and wish that filibustering could be handed over to the adept management of a trust but he could not get to the island and the war between Greece and Turkey swung to view with all the promise of a fine testing ground. "I am going to Greece for the *Journal*," he wrote, "and if the Red Badge is not all right I shall sell out my claim on literature and take up orange growing."

He was not without vanity and to be told, as he was constantly, that his book was mere fancy did not please him. To be told that he had imitated Zola's "Lâ Débâcle" probably pleased him less, as he disliked most of Zola's work. Even "Nana," that secret favourite of the American Puritan, bored him by its length although he found Nana herself amusing and, with his fatal lack of circumspection, informed a woman that "this girl in Zola is a real streetwalker.   I mean, she does not fool around making excuses for her career.   You must pardon me if I cannot agree that every painted woman on the streets of New York was brought there by some evil man.   Nana, in the story, is honest. . . . Zola is a sincere writer but—is he much good?   He hangs one thing to another and his story goes along but I find him pretty tiresome."

Effecting this irreverence casually he took orders from William Randolph Hearst and went off to England with a bad cold, having told Clyde Fitch that he would go on with their play when he came back from Greece. . . . The play had been a dozen times discussed and Fitch was impressed by the theme proposed.   But the two brains fell from each other on an obvious point.   There was to be this village in the Virginia of 1864 and the contentious armies would sweep in and out; a frightened young sentry would kill his best friend in the dark; a man would be afraid to touch a fallen body under orders to find papers in its pockets.   Yes, said Fitch, but, now, about a heroine?   Crane saw no woman concerned in this affair.   They argued in the vapour of Mouquin's while men came up to borrow money from their generosity helpless in the face of any claim by an old acquaintance but the mind back of Fitch's rather wistful mask of a French dandy was conventional.   A play without a "love interest" would never do. With all the playwright's atmospheric intelligence he was not daring outside small devices. His plays, alert, topical and vivid ran always in due form. He consented to the usual and never shook off the habit of the theatre even after success had piled about his anaemic body treasures of delicate furniture, of marmoreal surfaces shown against the lushness of purple velvet, of rare wines he could not use or relish in the slow starvation that rose from his earlier struggles to end his industry, his passions of gratitude and his respectful service to lovely women with pallid golden hair. . . . A curious miasma seemed to flow on all these Americans of that century's last decade. Their lungs broke and slew them. They were slaughtered by their brothers or by crazy musicians. Fame had picked up a dagger and made use of it at random, but no bores died young.

Crane's sketch of his arrival in London shows his defect as an artist for popular use. He lacked the easy sentimentalism which so grace the notes of other American writers who get to London but he saw a cab horse gravely slide down wet asphalt and was suddenly convinced that a man in a top-hat might be human. He had silently distrusted top-hats on Americans although their use was spreading and "there now exist many young men who consider that they could not successfully conduct their lives without this furniture. To speak generally I

should say that the headgear then supplies them
with a kind of ferocity of indifference. . . . Philosophy should always know that indifference is a
militant thing." He also saw the newest novel of
Hall Caine advertised on posters and startled William Heinemann by asking his English publisher if
England read Hall Caine's works. Crane may have
shared the purely American delusion that cheap novels are only read in the United States.

London contained, just then, dozens of American
correspondents and he could at once meet Harold
Frederic, principal agent of the *New York Times* in
England and, in 1897, the author of "The Damnation of Theron Ware," the sole courageous or truthful novel ever written by an American on the subject of religion. Frederic's fictions had changed, as
their maker changed, from simple romanticism to a
sort of shrewd, rough realistic tone and "Theron
Ware" had for Crane the precise appeal of familiar-
ity. He thought, privately, that "it could have been
written a darned lot better" but he liked the story of
the wavering young Methodist preacher who was bullied by sour old men of his stagnant church and
learned to like pleasure at the hands of some crude
hedonists who discharge their wisdom on Theron
Ware as encyclopedic lumps, terribly prophesying the
American novel of this moment. . . . Frederic's style
suggests the man's diverse personality. He was
shrewd, witty and assertive to a degree. Even a dear

friend would leave admissions that Frederic was not "finely fibred" and people who met him toward the end of a rather vexed life seldom much liked him, while his kindnesses to folk without importance and his desperate loyalties are as well remembered. He made many useful quips which survive in trans-mutations and borrowings. "Mr. Matthew Arnold plainly believes that Columbus should have been hanged in chains for the crime of discovering Amer-ica. . . . In the United States it is considered sin-ful to drink champagne and eat lobster after mid-night. Up to that hour it is a matter only of digestion. . . . Actresses are events which may take place in the most respectable family circles." His mind swung from balanced and liberal surveys to vehement prejudice and the one letter available to this study displays: "Mr. Edward Garnett [1] would be an El Dorado to an American publisher of the superior class. He seems to be able to scent a new talent in fiction from a thousand miles and as a critic he possesses both sincerity and distinction of manner. He should be made known to Ameri-cans. . . . 'The Red Badge of Courage' has prob-ably been successful in the U. S. more because it is a Civil War story than because it is a brilliant study of an individual. . . . Henry James is an effeminate old donkey who lives with a herd of other donkeys around him and insists on being treated as if he were

[1] He had no personal acquaintance with Mr. Garnett.

the Pope. He has licked dust from the floor of every third rate hostess in England. . . . Mr. James recommended Mr. Crane's novel before me in the house of our one mutual acquaintance and I was deterred from reading it for some days for that reason. With his usual lack of sense or generosity he described the book as an imitation of Zola's 'The Downfall' which it resembles as much as I do Miss Ellen Terry." His encounters with Henry James were infrequent but dreadful to people who preferred that the older man's gauzy periphery of sentiments and perceptual tenderness should remain unbruised. In 1895, for instance, Frederic listened while the novelist outlined a charming tour of cathedral towns to an American lady and then advised her to look through the slums of Liverpool and Manchester as well. . . . The florid, tall man haunted Ireland in hope of seeing a revolution start but, when a row began between peasants of his favourite fishing village and the British constabulary, he intervened. He abominated all the capacities of Oscar Wilde, but when the grand fakir was on trial, at last, refused to allow exaggerations to be sent to his newspaper and turned loudly on a group of gossips in a club with, "Why do you sit and lie about the poor devil when he's done for?" He had a war always threatening with any exquisite and some of his rudenesses were wondrous. "Your new book held me spellbound," he told a writer of thinly

charming essays who started to return thanks and
was halted by, "Yes, I rode clear past my station.
The guard had to wake me up at the next one."
Such wit belongs in the snuffbox of Talleyrand.
But Frederic had an honest, quite unaffected admiration for Crane and led him into the Savage on March
26th as though, says a witness, he had invented the
boy.

They appeared together at a luncheon given for
Crane by Richard Harding Davis on March 28th in
the Savoy and there Crane was presented to James
Barrie, Justin McCarthy, Anthony Hope and some
more. Frederic followed his new friend to Dover
and said good-bye on April 1st, giving him into the
keeping of Henry Sanford Bennett, a Canadian, on
his way to Greece also. Bennett spoke French and
guided Crane through Paris on April 2nd, making
discoveries about the silent American that ended
with a flash of Crane's disgust in Notre Dame where
some procession was passing toward the altar in
colour and music. Bennett was watching this ceremony when Crane pulled his arm and broke out, "I
can't stand that nonsense!" Colour, music and the
traditional pathos of mass made no excuse to his
nature for theatrical display. He looked with indifference at a review of cavalry but made Bennett
talk to a trooper for him about horses in the French
service and ask if the man had been at Gravelotte
in 1870. "He took," said Bennett, "not the slight-

est interest in any of the show places except the Luxembourg gardens and I had to help him talk to some French children there."

Paris never properly impressed Crane who spent his time on the way to Greece trying to master some phrases of French, suddenly worried because this war must be fought in strange tongues and he could speak only English. At Basle he mailed a letter: "I now know that I am an imbecile of rank. If nobody shoots me and I get back alive through those Indians in London I will stay home until there is a nice war in Mexico where it does not matter what you talk so long as you can curse immoderately. Willie Hearst has made a bad bargain." . . . He was right. Part of his prompt and flat failure as a war correspondent lay in his helplessness. He must rely on guides and interpreters throughout the brief campaign. The *New York Journal* and the *Westminster Gazette* had made a bad bargain. Even his sense of the comic straggled out under the blight and he could not well enjoy Athens with its masses of tourists who had come to see a real war comfortably. Notes of clear impression mingle with his reporting but his whole raid into Greece was a series of irritations and he wrote: "I guess that I expected some sublime force to lift me in air and let me watch. Well, no! Like trying to see a bum vaudeville show from behind a fat man who wiggles. I have not been well either."

He was not well and, given a practical nature, he would have resigned his post in Paris. Perpetual indigestion bothered him and he found the Greek food abominable. Meanwhile the crown prince Constantine had begun practice of his specialty by running away from combat to the disgust of all Greece and Crane arrived at Velestinos eight hours after the beginning of the great engagement that finished the war. He had gone plunging along the line of emptied hilltowns and villages that lay between Velestinos and Volo and came hurrying back with other stragglers to find Richard Harding Davis and John Bass the only American correspondents on the scene of the long duel between the ill officered Greek infantrymen and the agile Turkish force that peppered the trenches from an elevation. The war was lost, Davis accurately declared, in the cafés of Athens, and like Crane the expert raged at the command of the willing soldiers by dandies so ineffective. Davis went swiftly off to London and Crane, worn out, suffering from attacks of bowel trouble, strolled about Athens with Julian Ralph who marvelled finding that the impressionist knew nothing of Greek architecture and could not distinguish types of columns on the Acropolis.

Crane had no sense of line. His few attempts to draw a human shape are not even in proportion and the whole mass of his impressions, transcribed so brilliantly from a visible scene are truly "im-

pressions" and not careful photographs. He seldom
mentions contour in his quick passages of description. He saw the frenzied peasants rushing down
the mountain into Volo: "It was a freshet that
might sear the face of the tall, quiet mountain; it
might draw a livid line across the land, this down-
pour of fear with a thousand homes adrift in the
current—men, women, babes, animals. From it
there arose a constant babble of tongues, shrill,
broken, and sometimes choking, as from men drowning. Many made gestures, painting their agonies on
the air with fingers that twirled swiftly. The blue
bay with its pointed ships, and the white town lay
below them, distant, flat, serene." The people of
his tales have very seldom more than a suggestion
of body. A man has "indomitable whiskers" or
some clothes. The lad in "The Red Badge of
Courage," late in the book, has a bronzed throat.
The pretty girl of "The Third Violet" is simply
something the artist would like to paint—a trick of
entry that Crane left to some thousands of writers.
Since his art has lately been often likened to that
of Anton Tchehov with inevitable comments by
American critics as to his "able imitations" of the
Russian whose works were not, while Crane lived,
known outside Russia there is an interest in the
parallel but Crane never so elaborated his pictures
of people as did Tchehov in "The Steppes" and his
fullest description of a being is that of his brother's

setter, Chester, appearing as "Stanley" in "The
Third Violet." The contour of man had no particular spell for him and when he was asked to describe
Gertrude Kingston, the English actress who was his
choice as the prettiest woman on the London stage
he said, "Well, she's got black hair and a nose,"
which left James Huneker unenlightened.

These habits didn't prevent his enjoyment of
prolix or exact art. He valiantly argued with Julian
Ralph in Athens that "The Portrait of a Lady" was
a masterpiece. Tolstoy's "Anna Karenina" was "too
long because he has to stop and preach but it's a
bully book." He adored Tolstoy the superb and
ruthless artist but for Tolstoy the emotional peda-
gogue, the pilgrim of redemption, he had no use.
No fact so clearly sets Crane apart from Americans
of his day and shows the course of his damnation
by that criticism which still, for all the changing
tone of these last years, most resembles a wavering
lady in a dark crinoline, prudently girdled with
chaste iron. Scratch an American critic, says the
astute Julian Street, and you find a Yankee school-
marm. To that instructive gentlewoman Crane appeared as a rowdy little boy who brought dead mice
to school, a lurid and irregular child who upset the
other children and then ran off before he could be
taught on some filibustering game of his own making to leave a boy's cry trailing its shrill beauty
against the stupid night.

In tumultuous Athens, though, Crane was ill of a mild dysentary and was nursed by a fair, affable woman, older than himself, Cora Taylor, who had fallen in love with him at Jacksonville and had come after him to Greece. So writing from Paris on September 2nd, he told Sanford Bennett: "Frederic and Mr. Heinemann have been urging me to stay in England for a time. So my wife—after practicing nine days I can write that without a jump— and I will be hunting a house or an attic in London pretty soon."

VI

LONDON TO CUBA

AN American writer is safest abroad when he
has somewhere left in storage his entire critical sense and has for the voyage replaced it
by an emotional willingness comparable to the felicity
of a noticed puppy. He may then roam in his destined character giving neither pleasure nor offence to
men who will accept his admirations and hear his
raptures as mature women might accept the flowers
and phrases of some harmless schoolboy. On the
continent he will be, mostly, the child of the world's
milch cow but in England he must be wary as are
boorish relations of whose manners something too
much is known.

Crane's extreme dislike of Robert Louis Stevenson got him in trouble at William Heinemann's table
early in October when he recklessly or absently assured two of the dead Scot's correspondents that
Stevenson bored him. All through his first English
winter he was for ever meeting filaments of that monstrous reputation then being groomed for the American market by adoring hands. It had been well and
naturally established in England that "R. L. S." was

an American idol and a transatlantic who didn't admire may have seemed vastly affected. On October 12th Crane wrote: "I believe in ghosts. Mr. Stevenson has not passed away far enough. He is all around town."

There was another spook, in better flesh, whose reputation was not, in 1897 amenable to grooming. Literary London was shaken or amused by the rumour of memoirs being written in Reading Gaol by Oscar Wilde and Henry Harland, once an editor of "The Yellow Book" assured Crane that terrible things might be expected to happen if the collapsed dandy found a publisher for his book of memories. Crane again was bored. Only some passages of Wilde's plays had any interest for him and the poet in his view was just a sentimental neurotic who should be shipped for treatment to S. Weir Mitchell "or some other doctor who knows all about that kind of thing." He would later be shocked and nauseated by the sight of Wilde's blotched and powdered face bleating compliments at him in the smoke of the Café Procope but, now, his refusal to discuss Oscar as a splendid sinner irritated Harland sharply. A pet criminal is always sacred but Wilde had acquired a curious dignity because his case was restricted, in conversation, to small and liberal circles. In Crane's disgusted commentary: "Wilde was a mildewed chump. He has a disease and they all gas about

him as though there was a hell and he came up out
of it. . . . Mr. Yeats is the only man I have met
who talks of Wilde with any sense.   The others talk
like a lot of little girls at a Sunday School party
when a kid says a wicked word in a corner." Perhaps it was Crane's misfortune to be a little more
modern in 1897 than was necessary.   Or perhaps
a young man who had sat in tramp's clothes by
night in Union Square listening to darkened chatter
of real tramps might not be so thrilled over the
neurosis of an Irish poet.   His indifference to the
purple legend was disheartening.   He failed of taking Oscar Wilde seriously or sadly and that, too,
was held to be an affectation.

There was no tumult in the high world of letters
English because Stephen Crane had rented a villa
named Ravensbrook at Oxted in Surrey and proposed to make a stay.   He was even snubbed with
a vehemence that still bewilders the witnesses by
George Meredith on the steps of a club before Crane
had spoken to the celebrity.   Algernon Charles
Swinburne asked him to tea at Putney and, discovering that Crane neither read nor talked French,
entertained the American by translating bits of a
sixteenth century manuscript to him.   Extremely
sensitive to courtesies of men older than himself
Crane was still somewhat wearied by this cultivated
afternoon and spent the evening tramping with

Robert Barr through a slum not then well advertised in fiction, the Limehouse now illustrious and now, as then, very dull indeed.

He was so sensitive to attentions of people more ancient than Stephen Crane that the trait lends itself to psychiatric description. Many of his letters were written to two ladies fifteen years ahead of him, on whom he lavished luncheons in his prosperous spring of 1896. . . . They were both dyspeptic. He would turn from the prettiest girl in a crowded room to chat with an elderly lady. Favours of middle-aged folk had some special meaning for the final child of a long family, used to petting and scolding from brothers and sisters who had been longer living. When he was seventeen he doted on a Canadian gentlewoman with seven infants. At twenty-six he was ordered by James Huneker to read Balzac and only the contrary opinion of another authority stopped him. And now he was ordered by Harold Frederic to write a novel about his trip to Greece and, in November of 1897, he began it. Mr. Frederic thought he should, so he would. But "Active Service" somehow began itself slowly and lagged on his desk at Oxted while he took up other tales and finished "The Monster" one day in early December, having spent a whole week of interrupted evenings on the long story which shows every strength and every weakness of his armoury. Harold Frederic strolled over

from Robert Barr's house at Woldingham, within
sight of the dank villa grown already detestable to
Crane and, with Sanford Bennett, made an audience
for the reading aloud of the fantasy.

"The Monster" is a study of popular stupidity.
The foremost doctor of Whilomville restores to
life a vain negro hostler who has rescued his small
son from a burning house. Dr. Trescott's sentiment
keeps alive this fellow now an idiot and faceless.
The sentimentality of Whilomville has acclaimed
Henry Johnson a hero and a martyr while he was
thought dying. Now the kindly and aimless monster terrifies first the negroes who are paid to lodge
him, then a children's party, then his former
mistress, the belle of Watermelon Alley. The town
swings against the surgeon who has kept Henry
Johnson in being and the subject passes in vocal
exhibition through the gossip of the barber's shop
and through the kitchen wherein Martha Goodwin,
a woman who was nothing but the mausoleum of
a dead passion, gives judgment on the world's affairs and helps forward all local troubles by a
series of sniffs. The sermon on useless pity com-
pletes itself with the picture of Dr. Trescott counting unused teacups on his wife's neglected table.
Sentimentality has clubbed sentiment to death in
Whilomville. "The Monster" suffers from a defect
of exuberance; Crane's passion for recording fatuous
conversations reaches a height twice in the nar-

rative. The chatter in the barber's shop would not again be equalled for sheer emptiness until James Joyce wrote his "Portrait of the Artist as a Young Man" but it is dangerous to lay emptiness before emptiness without pointing out the vacuum and Crane's satire is implicit. To the taste of 1897, "The Monster" was plainly a horrible tale of a man who had no face and, when Paul Reynolds offered it to *The Century* it was refused with speed, an editor explaining to the puzzled agent, "We couldn't publish that thing with half the expectant mothers in America on our subscription list!" Even to Harold Frederic the story was offensive and he told Crane to throw it away. The other half of the audience, Mr. Bennett, promptly gave proof of the power of impressionism, deftly handled, as a mode in fiction. He was for years troubled by a memory of the negro's shattered visage and, picking up the tale after Crane died, was surprised to find that all his horror had been excited by the simple statement, "He had no face."

Crane thrashed up and down the room waiting for luncheon and arguing passionately while he tapped the butt of his Mexican revolver on furniture. What was wrong with people, anyhow? Here was a lot of ink on white paper and a story "with some sense in it." Why be frightened? His hopeless failure to catch the emotional viewpoint of average readers or, for that matter, of average writers came flashing up. "Men of sense" would not care if Henry Johnson had a face or no. The argument blazed. Mr. Bennett sat listening to the battle that lasted all through luncheon and ended in explosion. Frederic turned his guns on "The Nigger of the Narcissus" and Crane crashing down the revolver fatally on a dessert plate, yelled, "You and I and Kipling couldn't have written the Nigger!" Thus are these artists.

It has been worth while to detail this abstract quarrel since Crane was swiftly reported in New York as Harold Frederic's slave and subject. They were not seen so on November 30th by an American lawyer who called at Oxted. Next day he wrote to his wife: "Mr. (John) Stokes gave me a note of introduction to Mr. Crane and he was very pleasant in a quiet, boyish way when I got to his house. It surprised me how little he uses slang when his books are full of it and how young he is. Mrs. Crane asked me to stay for lunch. She is a southerner and very nice. I should imagine her to be six or seven years older than Mr. Crane with big blue eyes and reddish hair. Mr. Frederic, the *New York Times* correspondent came in the middle of the lunch with five other men and it was very embarrassing for Mrs. Crane as they were not expected. Mr. Frederic is not at all agreeable. He is funny in a sarcastic way about politics and people but he kept interrupting everybody else and was downright rude to Mr. Crane several times. They made Mr. Crane shoot with his revolver after lunch and he is a very fine shot. Some children came over from the next house to watch and Mrs. Crane made biscuit for tea. She is a wonderful cook."

By December a visible strain came on Crane's purse and Cora Crane's cookery. He wrote to Acton Davies: "Will you see if X—— and Y—— could let me have what they borrowed last May? I took X——'s note for $300 and Y—— owes me about $250. I hate to press nice fellows but it costs more to live over here than I was led to believe and some of these Comanche braves seem to think I am running a free lunch counter. Seven men have been staying over Sunday." So the plump little dramatic reporter ran Crane's errand in New York and failed to collect from men who hardly knew Crane and meanwhile parties of seven or, once, nine men came dropping down to convenient Oxted for Sundays of talk and poker. More game pies and claret must be sent for and, on December 3rd, he wrote: "I have been staying at this hotel"—it was Brown's, in Dover Street,—"two days so as to finish some work. Cora just now wires me that she has got rid of some people who have been boarding with us for three days, so I can go home."

He was, in short, pillaged by people who found his chromatic talk and his wife's biscuit admirable while his helpless good nature couldn't or didn't re-

pel visitors scarcely agreeable. At tea in John
Hay's house he told the Ambassador, after being
congratulated on his success, "I wish success paid
me a salary, sir," with a grin. In a few minutes,
the grin must have faded. A countess asked him
about his parents and when she heard that his
father had been a Methodist pastor broke into
laughter of some quality offensive to Hay and probably searing to Crane who thereafter recorded that
Lady Cardigan had no more manners than a streetwalker. This was, outside a small group of intimates, his last truthful statement as to his family
in England and a few days later he told a lady din-
ing beside him in the house of Hoyt De Fries that
his father was a Presbyterian Cardinal.

"Oh," said she, "do Dissenters have cardinals in
the States?"

The English unconsciousness of American habits
and customs did not annoy him but it entertained
him largely and he got an amusement out of wholesale lies: "They will believe anything wild or impossible you tell them and then if you say your
brother has a bathtub in his house they—ever so
politely—call you a perjured falsifier of facts. I told
a seemingly sane man at Mrs. Garnett's that I got
my artistic education on the Bowery and he said,
"Oh, really? So they have a school of fine arts
there?" I had, you see, just told Mrs. Garnett
while this mummy listened all about the Bowery—

in so far as I could tell a woman about the Bowery —but that made no difference to this John Bull. Now I am going to wave the starry flag of freedom a little—" (He was writing to Huneker)—"even if you contemn the practice in one who knows not Balzac and Dostoywhat'shisname. You Indians have been wasting wind in telling me how 'Unintrusive' and 'DELICATE' I would find English manners. I don't. It has not been the habit of people I meet at Mr. Howells or Mr. Phillips or Mrs. Sonntages to let fall my hand and begin to quickly ask me how much money I make and from which French realist I shall steal my next book. For it has been proven to me fully and carefully by authority that all my books are stolen from the French. They stand me against walls with a teacup in my hand and tell me how I have stolen all my things from De Maupassant, Zola, Loti and the bloke who wrote —I forget the book. I find nothing 'unintrusive' or 'delicate' in these goings on. The simple rustic villagers of Port Jervis have as good manners as some of the flower of England's literary set."

It was not believed in England that he was truly ill informed in letters and he tired of explaining that some books of criticism and a few paperbacked copies of Flaubert and De Maupassant in translation were his acquaintances, casually made, with the French nineteenth century. He had never read Stendhal's "La Chartreuse de Parme" and Henry

Harland's insistence that he MUST have read it before writing "The Red Badge of Courage" finally angered him. The journalists at the Savage were willing to take him as an amusing companion and the taverns of London were more interesting than drawing rooms where "everybody knows everybody else's business in the superlative degree and everybody reads everybody's books mainly—unless I am blind—to be at once able to tell everybody else how bad they are. Politics and literature have got wonderfully boiled into a kind of chowder. I feel like a clam."

Winter brought bad colds and a trip to Harold Frederic's pet Irish fishing village. On February 5th, he dined with Frederic and Charles Griswold, an American tourist, at Richmond. To this matrix of a pleasant evening were suddenly added a nobleman then in alliance with a lady never certain as to her nationality, understood to be the honoured subject of verses in "The Yellow Book" and reputed chaste though seldom sober. The party came back to Mr. Griswold's rooms in London and Madame Zipango—(the name is certainly international)—was imitating Yvette Guilbert when Henry James appeared to pay his young compatriot a call. The correct and the incorrect swam together in a frightful collision. Crane withdrew the elderly novelist to a corner and talked style until the fantastic woman poured champagne in the top hat of Henry James.

Her noble lover had gone to sleep. Frederic was amused. The wretched host of this group was too young and too frightened to do anything preventitive and Crane, coldly tactful, got the handsome creature out of the hotel, then came back to aid in the restoration of the abused hat.

Crane did not find this funny. In the next week he wrote: "I agree with you that Mr. James has ridiculous traits and lately I have seen him make a holy show of himself in a situation that—on my honour—would have been simple to an ordinary man. But it seems impossible to dislike him. He is so kind to everybody. . . ."

V He was so kind. From the sacred fount of his self-adoration there yet welled on gifted folk those pools of tender correspondence and those courtesies a trifle tedious, one hears, but rendered with such grace. Ada Rehan might vexedly call him "my dear snob" across a luncheon table but she would repent for weeks that bit of unpremeditated, natural frankness. Another actress, in a forgetful breath, assured him that she found his friend Paul Bourget's novels vulgar and then shook as the deep voice stammered, "Vul—" to begin some sentence of pained expostulation that ended in mere syllables of affront. He was no longer a man. Henry James was a coloured and complicated ritual that demanded of spectators a reverence unfailingly accorded. People who swooned under the burden of his final method sat and sat in pleasure while that astonishing egotism bared in slow phrases its detached and charming appreciation of its own singular skill. He had written plays incoherent and banal in exquisite English for the simple and admitted purpose of making money "as much and as soon as possible" and his votaries shuddered when the plebeians hooted "Guy Domville" from the stage. He committed in reviews consummate silliness such as his famous statement of tears shed over the butchered children of Rudyard Kipling's "Drums of the Fore and Aft" with its added comment on the dreadful dirtiness of the dead drummers. The sob balanced the snobbery and nobody jeered, save one remote and logical American. Critics mired themselves in verbal anguish over his successive novels. This plain and limited old bachelor commanded the world to respect him and the world obeyed. He was so kind.

Life waned for this man in his absurd and wonderful position, the patron of a cult. His books were so little read in America that he could be mentioned as "the late Henry James" in 1898 at a public banquet without exciting laughter. Americans invading England found, to their horror or secret relief, that nobody seemed to read his books in the territory assigned to his renown. But to no other writer in the Anglo-American field were attached such bristling adherents! He was holy and impeccable

to the gaze of innumerable talented folk. Mrs.
Humphry Ward fell speechless and scarlet when it
was said, in her presence, that Mr. James had derived his tale "Paste" from De Maupassant and
another votary still living ordered from his house
a heretic who chose to argue that the Master's pre-
occupation with refinements was a vulgar habit. He
was prim and circumspect, as befitted the child
grown old who was ordered at the age of seven to
compose a note of apology for appearing barefoot
on the porch of a seaside villa before callers, and
he was the pet of cynical voluptuaries. He was a
provincial sentimentalist touted by worshippers as
the last flower of European culture while he recoiled
in amazement from the profound civilization of
Havelock Ellis who would and, "so successfully
delicate in his attack on the matter of these abominations that one reads, I may say, almost pain-
lessly," did write of sexual deflections and gross
social phenomena without any sign of shock. This
fading life of Henry James had passed in a series
of recoils. Civilization, in his sight, seems to have
been not the overthrow of empty inhibitions but an
exaltation of limits. He had fled—and who blames
him?—from a society that became, in his dreams, a
tentacled beast ready always to overpower his individual trend but he remained a Bostonian by
every implication of his rare and scrupulous art.
Even when in "The Turn of the Screw" he attempted

to tell the story of "abominations" he must produce
it with ghosts for sinners and the corrupted bodies
must be those of children impossible and lovely as
the babes of his predecessor Hawthorne. This master of groomed circumstance had found out a sunny
garden where poisons blew as perfumes too heavy
for a refined sense and crimes were shadows, not
clouds, that swept across his shaved and watered
turf.

Destiny now jolted the European sod beneath the
feet of loitering transatlantics. On the night of
February 15th the battleship *Maine* was blown up
in the harbour of Havana and in two days it was
known that treachery was suspected by the American government. The world's press went mad with
all the brilliance of its eternal parochialism and any
student in popular misinformation may gather material of delicious merits from the abiding files.
Henry James was distressed by the "seeming inac-
curacy of the Parisian, or indeed of all the Continental reports" and Stephen Crane was bored at
once to hear that "American troops always run at
the first shot and there is no such thing as the U. S.
Navy. These matters were clearly proven to me
last night at the Savage by a Mr. Wyndham who
once met General Grant. I have vainly tried to tell
some good men and true that Cuba is not on friendly
terms with California but they will have it that one
gets on a tug at San Francisco to go to Havana."

He took the end of the *Maine* so calmly that some
of his friends were appalled. The quality of his
·nature forbade outcries after an event and his "fatal-
ism" seems rather to have been a severe reticence
in the sight of disasters. The American colony in
London grew hysteric and John Stokes reproached
Crane with his coolness while the English press as-
sumed an indignant tone and in Paris, *La Patrie* invented a formula of objections. Were the com-
patriots of Cervantes and Velasquez to be accused
of sinking a warship in time of peace? Some emotional incantation, now unknown, summoned up
Velasquez and Cervantes as the Castor and Pollux
of the moment in aid of Spain. These artists were
invoked ceaselessly and jumped the Channel. . . .
All at once Americans discovered themselves to be
the dogs of the universe. The issue was confused
by the report of the Commission which investigated
the sinking of the *Maine* and with a certainty neither
graceful nor diplomatic experts French, English and
German in the capitals of those lands asserted that
the Commission lied in all its findings. Dislike of
the United States turned journals formerly loud in
their insistence that the United States should inter-
vene on behalf of Cuba. Alternately Spain was a
tottering lady to be defended from the assaults of
a brutal ruffian or a proud power capable of sweeping American fleets and troops from the map with
one gesture. The press of America was silly in its

brashness and the press of Europe was silly from contempt long hoarded in its editorial brain. The spectacle was repeated, of course, later but its vividness in 1898 bewildered the Yankee and roused the Southerner. In Europe the nose of the golden calf was slapped with such violence that the poor beast began, not without primitive reasons, to turn and canter lowing homeward. On March 10th landlords in Paris were quaintly worried by the flight of Americans from a city in which they were daily insulted and the proprietors of hotels addressed themselves in some agitation to the newspapers. Tinkling harshly, the dollar rolled away from the scene of its worship and cynics were diverted by the minatory sound. . . . The American's one value was in motion, and vulgar, acutely sensitive to that noise, Joseph Chamberlain advised, "Care should be taken that the American financial authorities do not take offence."

Another excitement shook London in the middle of March. Paying huge prices for stalls the smart world went in its best coat to see a benefit arranged for Nellie Farren, crippled and penniless in her discarded age. Magnificents who had refused to contribute a pound to her comfort now blubbered duly in boxes while the little paralytic was borne on the stage to croak her thanks. Henry Irving kindly recited "The Dream of Eugene Aram" and Ellen Terry loosed the enchantment of her voice as Ophelia.

Marie Tempest sang a ballad from "The Geisha"
and a whole train of celebrated actresses deployed
their graces before Crane whose evening dress
was painfully tight, he wrote, but "Oscar Hammerstein couldn't get people to make bigger fools
of themselves.   Except Willie Hearst nobody under-
stands the popular mind as well as Oscar.   I see no
difference between the *Journal* and Hammerstein's
roofgarden.   You get the blonde with the tincan in
her gullet and the comic speaker and the song about
mother's wayward boy in both shows.   I must affil-
iate with Hammerstein.   Mr. Conrad and I are
writing a new kind of play."

But, in Washington, the senator from Vermont
had read his dry, emotionless report on the condition of Cuba and in a bar of Broadway some man
lowered his glass with the wavering sentence, "Gentlemen, remember the *Maine!*"   Imperfect history
tells us only that he had a red moustache but war
was now inevitable and, for once, his court turned
unbelieving eyes on Mark Hanna when he grunted
that Spain could be licked in six months.   The assistant Secretary of the Navy paused before resigning
his post to frustrate the revealed wish of some fifty
Methodist and Baptist preachers in self-appointed
committee that all Roman Catholic chaplains be
withdrawn from ships sent to action, then went off
to gather a regiment of cavalry.   With parade and
consequence promptly recorded in the social col-

umns hundreds of well-washed New Yorkers offered
their services to their country and bloody squadrons
sailed in print from Cadiz to ravage the American
seaboard with guns of a calibre not yet found. . . .
Whether the nation was preparing to avenge the
Maine or to free Cuba was quite uncertain in the
nation's mind but somebody was going to suffer and
Crane wrote: "This war will be fought in English.
I can at least swear in Spanish and it will be more
comfortable all around.   But I have not decided on
going yet."

He was ill.   After a cerebral hemorrhage Harold
Frederic was dying, so consciously that he lifted
aside a corner of the handkerchief partly veiling
his distorted face to wink at callers who told him
he would soon be well again.   And, dying, the
hedonist accepted Christian Science treatment to
please a devoted woman who was made a scandal
in the press with all the usual vulgarities attendant
on an erratic and published man's vanishing.   He
had taken close hold on Crane's affection, though,
and the younger American lingered.   Then, suddenly, he left a note at Sanford Bennett's rooms:
"Sorry not to have seen you.   I have raised the
wind and sail tomorrow.   Nothing I can do for
Harold.   Barr will look after him.   Write me at
Hartwood, N. Y., care of Edmund Crane.   Shall get
myself taken in the Navy if possible."   He was so
swiftly out of England that guests came down to

Oxted and were surprised to find him gone. Only
after he sailed *The World* cabled to secure his
services and he did not present himself at the office
in New York until a Naval recruiting bureau had declined his body.   Then he was off to Key West where
Sampson's fleet pivoted on the mangy little city filled
with journalists, harlots and mosquitoes who all
found a nightly meeting place in the gambling hell.
Thence came to Robert Barr a letter postmarked
May 23rd: "You should see the jay who runs the
table here.   He is straight out of a dime novel,
moustache and all, with bunches of diamonds like
cheap chandeliers on each hand.   Now I owe Harold
an apology for laughing when he said they would
tear me in pieces the minute my back was turned.
Hi, Harold!   I apologize!   Did you know me for
a morphine eater?   A man who has known me ten
years tells me that all my books are written while
I am drenched with morphine.   The joke is on me."
But the gambling hell was delightful and he took
notes of its owner's conversation.   The man knew
easily, he said, nine hundred distinct oaths.   When
he told bawdy tales the ceiling changed colour and
his sarcasm was so theatrically effective that it appears too theatrical in "Moonlight on the Snow."
This character must be made use of in the play and
Crane's character was blighted more deeply while he
lounged, pointed out to strangers, in the smoky
rooms already hot with tropical spring.   He missed

the fleet's bombardment of Matanzas but once the
flagship carried him so closely by the breakers
lazily flapping crystal foam on the island's sands
that he could see a naked child tossing its hands
in welcome from the shore.

VII

CHANGE

THAT irrelevant baby becomes a convenient
symbol of Crane's doubled nature. He still
wanted to push his growing frailty against
the random gestures of society's bad behaviour. He
would be in the middle of matters with which, as an
artist, he found himself concerned. Sense and the
warnings of friends should have kept him away
from Cuba but his curiosity took him there quite inevitably. The man had not yet learned certain high
values of posture: as a superior writer he should have
sentimentalized his position, retiring gravely into
an attitude but the elaborate fustian of his profession
had no charm for him at the age of twenty-six and
here was this comprehensible war to be heard in
English with many of his comrades impatient at Key
West or dodging in despatch boats after Sampson's
fleet as it swept along the island's northern coast. So
he appeared and won three hundred dollars from the
estimable gambler in intervals of slow cruising on
the tug *Three Friends* with a bundle of manuscript
and the worst equipment for a campaign ever seen.

He was at once wonderfully disliked by some men who here saw Stevie Crane for the first time. Travel and reputation had not made him less reserved and he gave no proper account of his stay in England. England was all right. He had met some bully people. No, he hadn't seen much of Rudyard Kipling and while he found James Barrie a nice fellow he did not praise the new favourite's work. There was a prompt impression of chilly listlessness and to a young gentleman who told him how greatly he resembled Robert Louis Stevenson Crane straightway answered, "I hope I outgrow it," and that, too, was not diplomatic. Old friends thought him little changed and his poker was as bad as ever.

The war now halted while Europe took care to revise its opinion of the American navy after Dewey massacred a feeble collection of Spanish gunboats in Manila Bay. Lord Salisbury paraphrased for the Primrose League, on May 4th, some ideas of Friedrich Nietzsche as to dying states and the rights of the stronger nations. Crane grinned a good deal over the new tone in despatches from abroad and went one day quickly to look at the sandy camping place appointed for troops gathering at Tampa in the rising temperature of May's last weeks. There he cast an eye on volunteer regiments assembling and disgusted correspondents by one of his usual failures in enthusiasm. The volunteers had forsaken their business and already underwent the hardships of the soldier without complaint. This was plainly noble of the volunteers but Crane affronted a group by asking, "Don't the militia take an oath to defend the country anyhow?" and only Frederic Remington joined him in this negative state of mind while the woes of the militia were telegraphed daily to journals which either suppressed the details or began, as no battles occupied front pages, to make a cause against the laborious Alger, Secretary of War, who was following the routine of his task and giving proper orders never strictly obeyed. Crane gave a lad from Wisconsin, discharged for heart trouble without any means of leaving Tampa, the necessary fifty dollars for his fare, then went back to Key West and the despatch boat's motion on a sea now troubled by mythical Spanish keels. Admiral Cervera's swift squadron had eluded Commodore Schley and lay serene in the harbour of Santiago but Admiral Camara's monstrous armament was roaming in the sophisticated press of New York and old ladies of Nantucket Island were agitated by glimpses of smoke on the horizon.

"The sailormen of Sampson's big canoe," Crane wrote from the *Three Friends* on June 2nd, "ought to make us all ashamed of our trade. The papers come aboard the flagship and who, I ask, want to see this goulash of legendary lies and solemn rumours? We do, we the cynics of Fleet Street and Park Row, the Rudyards, the lords of the popular mind. The Jackies just look at all this manure and say, Well—and go on polishing brass. Davis and I tried to make them excited by donations of headlines and they said, Well—and peeled more onions. It is now the fashion of all hotel porches at Tampa and Key West to run Davis down because he has declined a captaincy in the army in order to keep his contract with his paper. The teaparty has to have a topic."

Other topics being scarce, he revised a story called "Vashti in the Dark" which tells how a young Methodist preacher from the South killed himself after discovering that his wife had been ravished by a negro in a forest at night. To Acton Davies who typed the manuscript, this was one of Crane's best tales but no magazine ever bought it and Crane burned it in one of his rare fits of pique. Now he was struck by a title for a novel—"The Merry Go Round." This would be the adventures of a wandering carrousel in the Southwest and along the Atlantic shore. Projects boiled in him while the tug rocked and was nearly mangled by the *U. S. Machias* one hot night. James Pinker, his English agent, was paying forty pounds for each thousand words of his prose, so there might be a trip around the world, because "a Polish friend of mine who is an unancient mariner says I would be dippy over Polynesia." Meanwhile, he lounged and wondered, with crescent boredom, how to make an end of "Active Service" and out of that contemplation, rose a remark on a postcard: "A reporter is no hero for a novel."

He came to the decision at the wrong second of journalistic history.   In Tampa some reporters were doing the heroic thing.   The process of vision had brought revolt and offices in New York were bothered by facts, facts of all sorts, written and wired from the buzzing luxury of the hotel where ladies following chastely that odd camp danced under coloured lights.   Windy patriotism and romance were collapsing into hot veracity.   The men of the press saw a willing army ill fed, badly dressed for a climate grown tormenting and made ready for transport in ships hardly fitted to carry uncritical cattle.   John Jacob Astor was offering to pay, since the Government wouldn't, for a decent supply of water and many eyes saw the beginning of a crime on men rendered defenceless by discipline.   The nation had engaged in a sentimental war and whooped at home for news of bloodshed.   The symbol of Tampa was a rocking chair in cartoons and already Major General Shafter was complaining of his health to the attachés of Germany and Great Britain.   Back from Florida spread a humming noise of discontent.   The regular Army was worthless.   The war ought to be turned over to the volunteer officers directly.   Everything was wrong.   The papers said so.

On June 10th six hundred Marines landed from a bevy of gunboats on the eastern bank of Guantanamo's charming bay below Santiago and the despatch tug shed Crane with the force, enchanted by the glow of a burning village whence a fiery light was thrown upon some palms and "made them into enormous crimson feathers." The Marines in tawny linen uniforms camped on a flat plateau that interrupted this steep shore and Crane talked all night long to a surgeon named Gibbs about consumptions while trenches were dug. Men were annoyed by the active Cuban land crab's scuttling on their faces as they slept. Next afternoon, while they bathed in squads from the littered beach, firing began suddenly and Cuban scouts brought word that the guerillas were the marksmen. Naked Marines and dressed Marines shot for an hour against the dense, lustrous green of the jungle and night came with vehemence while Crane lugged water up the hill, canteens rattling by the dozen from shoulders that already shivered. The surgeon gave him quinine and advised flight. The *Three Friends* had sailed to Jamaica but Gibbs wanted the sick man to take shelter on the *Marblehead* or some other gunboat. . . . No. He had come to see this war and the correspondents of the despatch boat had let him stay to see it. Volleys scattered on the plateau where men sprawled in hot blackness and Crane crouched part of the doleful time beside the signalman who waved slow lanterns sending word to the *Marblehead* how things went on this knob. The lights drew fire from the brush that on three sides flowed near the poor entrenchments and the guerillas conversed between shots in the song of the local wood-dove. Then a ball struck the surgeon Gibbs and he began audibly to die in the crowded darkness while other wounded men cried out. Crane lay listening. . . . "Every wave, vibration, of his anguish beat upon my senses. He was long past groaning. There was only the bitter strife for air which pulsed out into the night in a clear, penetrating whistle with intervals of terrible silence in which I held my own breath in the common unconscious aspiration to help. I thought this man would never die. Ultimately he died." The next noon when Ralph Paine landed from the returned tug with a flask of whiskey Crane had an illusion of his tall friend as Harold Frederic in a fur coat and neither whiskey nor fresh food cleared the thought from his brain for hours. Perhaps one does not jam the colour of life on a feverish intelligence stoked with quinine harmlessly. He had no belief in ghosts and arguments on the immortality of the soul were dull to him as Presidential speeches but now people began to remind him of the dead. Caspar Whitney was like his father and he soon startled Harding Davis by telling the big man he was a corpse seen at Velestinos.

On June 14th the parties of Marines advanced into the jungle and swept the Spanish sharpshooters before them, burning a blockhouse and its heliograph

with a water tank named Cuzco from a village that
had been. The *Dolphin* shelled the woods ahead
of the column and Crane was vexed by another
illusion, transmuted in "War Memories" to a mere
comparison. He was shooting with his brothers at
Hartwood and the bursting shells were setters that
roused birds. He ran errands for the lieutenant in
charge of this fantastic sport and got official notice
of his coolness under fire. Then the *Three Friends*
carried him off from four days' piled strain to Port
Antonio and, he hoped, to fine meals. But the re-
sources of the small neutral port were scanty and the
chemist had only one toothbrush in stock. "This
town," he wrote, "is disgustingly ill appointed."

He made a tour around the Spanish outposts and
saw, guided by half-clad Cuban scouts, the squadron
of Cervera anchored in the round bay of Santiago as
he cowered in the brush above the packed town
wherein yellow fever had sprouted. It was a ride
of almost forty miles, coming and going through
danger, but "I did not discover my condition until we
were well through the Spanish lines and . . . then
I discovered I was a dead man. The nervous force
having evaporated I was a mere corpse. My limbs
were of dough and my spinal cord burned within me
as if it were a red hot wire." But he must tramp the
beach at Daiquiri and watch the troops land from
transports commanded mostly by insolent or cow-
ardly civilians who flouted the signals of General

Shafter's orders and sailed tranquilly out to the supreme safety of open water with medicines and necessary equipment in the holds of the shipping hired at such colossal rates by the government. The tragedy of the Santiago campaign had well begun and confusions heaped themselves on heat while Crane investigated the American regular officers, those curios of a system which immured boys for four years in a military monastery, sent them to duties in petty forts and barren towns of the vanished frontier and then produced their weariness for a public which at once expected of them diplomacies, social censorship and the suave attitudes of a society that exiled and disregarded them until the instant of its need.

The commanding officer of this little army was a fat invalid who reposed on a cot and whined about his health. In gayer hours he told anecdotes that shocked both Richard Harding Davis and Acton Davies by the flavour of medical information contained in his style. Apparently the man was too sickly or too careless for any exercise of will and after the neatness of the landing Major General Shafter simply vanished from the beautiful beach while his veteran subordinates did what they could to make life better and brighter for twelve thousand men sweating in shirts of thick wool and in a temperature wavering between eighty and a hundred degrees. Dismounted cavalrymen and the hard infantrymen called sometimes "doughboys" bathed their mosquito bites in saltwater wondering why the commissariat was already short of tobacco. . . . From the camp of the First Volunteer Cavalry arose the pulsating voice of Theodore Roosevelt demanding food and clean drink for that amazing regiment of tramps, actors, cowboys, expert bartenders, millionaires and football players. From the camp of the journalists rose the anguish of the *World's* chief correpondent as Crane didn't turn in his highly paid prose for the cable to jerk in edited sentences to New York. The terrible infant was loose among the regiments delighted with so much to see and hear.

He saw almost nothing of the battle known as Las Guasimas on June 24th, a tortuous raid through two converging trails carried out by Wheeler's brigade. As usual, Richard Harding Davis had the best of that news. The thing envied as "the Davis luck" was rather a very swift, shrewd judgment of possibilities and Davis followed Roosevelt while unseen Spaniards in the metallic prettiness of the foliage killed some Rough Riders. Crane ran three miles to overtake Young's dismounted troopers on the other trail and presently ran back six miles to Siboney without stopping to survey the end of this action. His friend Edward Marshall had been shot through the body, so the war lost all charm while Crane tried to get help from the *Journal's* staff at the beach. Then he guided some sailors with a cot for the wounded man and

walked beside this improvisation to Siboney again.
That night he could not eat but he shocked Henry
Carey and Acton Davies by saying it must be interesting to be shot.   He had noticed that men struck
in the chest ran ahead for a while before falling.   Ab-
dominal wounds crumpled the recipient.   Davies was
in the last miseries of sunburn.   His rotundity always appeared to be coated with pink celluloid and
he was now the tint of boiling lobster speckled by
huge blisters.   Crane stopped pouring linseed oil on
the misplaced dramatic reporter's shoulders and
mused, "You'd look bully if a shell hit you, ol' man.
Like a squashed peony."   The comparison was not
kind and Davies took alarm.   Crane seemed to want
to be hit and talked academically of locations on his
person for a bullet's entry.

He certainly went about the business of risking a
wound with extraordinary and scientific zeal.   Bri-
gades pushed on in the riotous jungle and stretched
thinly on July first before lizard-shaped crests up-
holding the villages of El Caney and San Juan.
These hills were a necessity to the Spanish defence.
Santiago could be shelled at leisure of the invaders
if the range of steep slopes and delusive plateaus fell
to the Americans.   General Vara Del Rey bravely
commanded the force at El Caney and there he was
killed in a ferocious little battle that lasted for nine
hours.   The San Juan fight was less venomous but
more trying.   Regiments sat in hollows or hasty

trenches while the Spanish fire came sputtering down-hill and the road rearward was a muddle of wounded men, advancing columns and, for a while, of strug-gling horses as the few guns were brought up to shell the enemy's position. Intolerable heat, windless and constant, lay on this episode as Crane walked to and fro in a grey, conspicuous English waterproof, afraid to shed the coat because he might lose it. When he appeared with James Hare strolling along the line of Wheeler's brigade at noon the cavalrymen lifted their heads and begged him to wear furs if he wasn't hot enough.

Crane brooded, staring up the hill and stooped once or twice to look at the holes made by bullets landing near his feet in the bleached grass of the slope. He wandered close to a depression that didn't greatly shelter Leonard Wood and Richard Harding Davis. It seemed to Davis that the pale coat drew shots. Yellow sand flicked from the trench and soldiers called to Crane, swearing uncomfortably. His specu-lation became interminable and the Spanish officer who paraded the defending trenches with a walking stick once visibly aimed it at the artist. This un-known warrior pleased Crane immensely and many other reporters tried afterwards to find the man's rank or name. But his pleasure in the spectacle was interrupted by Davis who yelled to him and bade him lie down. "Crane jumped," Davis reported, "as if he was waking from a nap and looked at me

astonished by my voice, perhaps. He flattened out
on the grass and crawled back behind a small hillock.
But pretty soon he rose on his knees and then stood
up once more, absorbed in watching. I called out
as sarcastically as I could that Colonel Wood and I
were not impressed by his courage and he blushed
scarlet before he lay down. He did not stay long
after that but helped a wounded man back to the
battery at El Poso. . . ." The third point of the
narrative was omitted by Davis. Colonel Wood
moved away and Crane got up for the second time.
Davis also rose, stepped over some prostrate soldiers
and caught Crane by the shoulders, forcing him
down. A bullet knocked off Davis's hat and the
leather of his field glass was chipped by another ball.
Then Crane went to play his game elsewhere and
drank some coffee at the reporters' camp behind a
battery that slung shells toward the Spanish blockhouse. He came back as the soldiers struggled up
the hill and was seen trying to hammer back a loose
heel of his shoe while the American flag was swung
over the conquered village. Night and desolation
smothered the battlefield while officers wrangled as
to the safety of holding the crests and Leonard Wood
reverted to his primary profession in the hospital, un-
dermanned, packed with dying youth. Another step
had been taken in the publicity of Theodore Roosevelt. Santiago was lost, although nobody quite understood so, and a corporal shot through both arms

sat up in a corner of the stinking tent reserved to fevers, singing "The Star Spangled Banner" with irony, at the top of his voice.

Chill winds belied the date and rain fell in long showers on the camps now stretched twelve miles from the beach to the taken hills. Days passed and Crane found that life without doses of whiskey and quinine was mere haze. He lurched off to see refugees from the city straggle into El Caney and to watch a surgeon operate on wounded Spanish soldiers in the chapel. He saw Richmond Hobson come between the regiments standing hatless in honour of his release and watched the hero of the *Merrimac* bow profusely as men pressed around him but this welcome was his last sight of the idle army waiting outside Santiago. Crane was now a figure of irresponsible sickness. His friends tried to feed him and kept him sometimes quiet but he wandered on a pony from place to place in the lines and lamented that he had missed the destruction of Cervera's fleet on July 3rd. He had gone to Jamaica with the despatch boat for a bath and some decent food. When the *Three Friends* brought him back, there were Sampson's grey ships in their usual place and the invincible Spanish squadron was already beginning to rust with tropical swiftness on the beach.

All sorts of fever had broken out in the American camp. Crane was apparently no more ill than were a dozen other reporters and photographers. People who spoke to him often thought him merely drunk. Then suddenly he was very plainly delirious all one night and Sylvester Scovel hauled him down to a ship loading with sick at Daiquiri. Crane was in a state of alternate vapour and lucidity. He sat on Scovel's pony chatting to Henry Carey and George Rhea gaily and then began to beg for pickles. Fever had dowered him with two yearnings—orange ice cream soda and sour pickles. Rhea saw the wreck taken aboard the transport and Crane was ordered to isolate himself as a case of yellow fever. He lay on a rug, aft, and was fed casually on stewed tomatoes. Cuba vanished from him in an opalescent languor while wounded negroes chanted jubilee as the ship sailed westward.

He had not yellow fever, actually, but the accumulated fatigue of twenty mad days had smitten him. It can only be a theory but Crane had long shown symptoms of intestinal consumption. Improperly or too coarsely fed he was ill and in Cuba he had relied on stimulants from July 1st to July 7th. In order to meet the procession of the *Merrimac's* crew at San Juan Hill he swallowed half the content of Carey's brandy flask and as soon as his brain drank in the show, he let himself flop on the grass, asleep at once. Scovel and Rhea tried to feed him but everything save soft fruit was an abomination. He could not even ride the Jamaican polo pony and men who had heard of his marvellous horsemanship saw the gaunt adventurer tumble from the saddle. Crane made his body a testing ground for all sensations of living and for this most un-literary habit he paid, in the useful language of melodrama, the price.

A representative gathering of Americans now saw the physical bill of their emotional war. Cuba was freed. The transport floated to the pier at Old Point Comfort and Crane was allowed to go ashore directly. The hotels of the resort were jammed with women— wives of naval and military officers, fashionable ladies from New York, curious tourists or anxious waiters. On the verandah of Chamberlain's Hotel he bowed to Mrs. Bolton Chaffee who had dined at Oxted three months before. She did not know the wraith in soiled khaki, hatless and unshaven, and her small grandson was scared to tears but after recognition she tried to get Crane to bed. No. He sat smoking on the arm of her chair and drawled sarcasms. Here is what he wanted to see: "The verandah was crowded with women in light, charming summer dresses and with spruce officers from the fortress. It was like a bank of flowers. It filled me with awe. . . . Across the narrow street on the verandah of another hotel was a similar bank of flowers. Two companies of volunteers dug a lane through the great crowd of the street and kept a way, and then through this lane there passed a curious procession. I had never known that they looked like that. Such a gang of dirty, ragged, emaciated, half starved and bandaged

cripples I had never seen. . . . Then there were many
stretchers, slow moving.   When the crowd began to
pass the hotel the banks of flowers made a noise which
could make one tremble . . . something beyond
either a moan or a sob.   Anyhow the sound of women
weeping was in it—   The sound of women weeping."

Of course he went back to see the orderly, almost
bloodless taking of Porto Rico and accepted the sur-
render of a rural village in which he was found the
next morning drilling children on the principal
street.   Mrs. Chaffee was seen with him at Old Point
so naturally it was reported in New York that Crane
had eloped with the wife of General Chaffee and was
living in adulterous splendour at San Francisco.
General Chaffee had no wife possible for this purpose
but Crane wrote to Mrs. Bolton Chaffee: "You must
be careful about feeding runaway dogs.   Mr. Bemis
informs me that you and I are sinners and that we
have flown to San Francisco.   They have promoted
you to the rank of Mrs. Brigadier General Chaffee.
Perhaps it is not known to you—and it has not long
been known to me—that my name in New York is
synonymous with mud.   Give my regards to your
husband and tell him the cigars made many correspondents happier.   My friends will pile a mountain
of lies on me but they will smoke my cigars as freely
as I smoke theirs.   That is cynicism."

Accused promptly of cynical coldness as to the
war, his real mood was the usual indifference to cheap

sentiment tied with amazingly frank admission of his
liking for certain exhibits. He was mute on Theodore Roosevelt's conduct as a commander in battle
and positively lyric as to his care for the Rough
Riders: "Say, this fellow worked for his troopers
like a cider press. He tried to feed them. He helped
build latrines. He cursed the quartermasters and
the—"dogs"—on the transports to get quinine and
grub for them. Let him be a politician if he likes.
He was a gentleman, down there." Admiral Sampson's coolness of manner did not distress him, as it
did other correspondents. But the commanders had
scant interest for him. The men, the utterly commonplace privates and recruits absorbed him. "Yes,
yes I know that it has been wonderfully proven how
that the doughboys and the Jackies know nothing of
manorial architecture and Pierre Loti. They care
not if the journal of the sisters De Goncourt is never
published at all. Velasquez? No. Cervantes?
No. United intellects of superior lands bade them
be licked to the glory of Cervantes and Velasquez.
I don't know why. I shall never know why. But
there is an excellence of human conduct independent
of Cervantes and Velasquez. The Spaniards who
lay dead in El Caney knew something of it. Our men
knew something of it. Mob-courage?—mob-courage. The mob has no courage. That is the chatter
of clubs and writers. Pray go stand with your back
to deadly fire from a painted drop for a pantomime

and wave signals for half an hour without wincing and then talk of mob-courage. Imperialism? All right. The White Man's Burden? What in hell did Private Jones and Seaman Smith know of it? Stop being sarcastic. A year hasn't diminished by one inch my respect for the men. I shall never see another war. I don't care if Buller drives all the Boers up Egypt's fattest pyramid. The men were all right."

His own posture in "War Memories" is that of a nervous and embarrassed spectator at an imbecile and ill-rehearsed show but he chooses no such attitude for the soldiers in "The Price of the Harness" or elsewhere in the sketches of the little campaign. There was lacking in Crane that profound and diffused sentimentalism that turns an individual reaction into an universal woe. It was impossible for a being who had lived in the Bowery by night and watched the ferocious diversions of San Antonio's Mexican quarter to whimper over mud and sweat and pain. War was ridiculous but men went to war. He accepts the visible with small protest. . . "What were we doing there at all? There was no definition. There was no use in quoting Tolstoy. There was no Napoleon to say the right thing and lend a gilded finish to the occasion. It galled one's mind at times. But there we were." It seemed best to accept the situation with calm raillery, to notice that a dying man could vex his friends by peevishness and that "the sun threw orange lances over enamelled, broad leaves."

He now fell in love with Havana and so sat writing there when he should have gone back to England. Some shadowy person named "Wells," not to be confused with H. G. Wells, had informed the woman anxious in Surrey of Crane's adultery with the mythical general's lady. A theme had occurred to him. The past was wooing Crane more vividly than it did in his first years. Havana, lazy and filthy, suggested a tale of old days. Suppose that a young sailor was cast up naked on the shore of Cuba and became the lover of a Spanish lady in the coloured, lascivious city? But he could get no clear account of Cuban history and Spanish was unreadable. The story was abandoned and he finished "Active Service" before starting North, then threw the last chapters aside and wrote them afresh. In October he got to New York after a stay in Washington where again he considered Congress from its gallery and again it bewildered him. He was presented to some Senator who told him gravely about the failures of the war and the discomforts undergone by a nephew in the Rough Riders. "I understand, now, that Congressmen and Senators all rolled in august pain by night and sat weeping by day over our lot. This warhorse told me so. He told me that he visited the War Department hourly on July First. I asked

him what good that did and he said it showed his
interest in the campaign. Nobody would believe in
him. I can't believe in him but it is true that I saw
him."

New York received him with a faint but noted
noise. His arrival was announced. Crane exposed
himself in Cuba no more recklessly than did Edward
Marshall, H. T. Whigham or George Rhea but he
had been officially mentioned and Harding Davis had
already before the public his article on the correspondents. Frederic Stokes was anxious for a novel
and accepted another book of verses. Editors were
offering higher rates. Paul Reynolds could sell "The
Blue Hotel" for as much as three hundred dollars, a
price almost as high as those accorded to Davis or
Kipling. But Crane was off to Hartwood at once
and his brothers were appalled by a condition suddenly manifest. The man was ill and restless. He
rode and shot with vigour but listlessness had come
on him. People at Port Jervis crowded to hear him
talk or to tell him stories he should write and he
played long games with his nieces. Yet something
had happened. The vitality of manner was gone; he
slept endlessly; he put off necessary visits to New
York. He was too tired to breathe, he wrote, and
when William Dean Howells gave a luncheon for
him at Delmonico's he sat silently respectful among
older men, eating nothing, turning the stem of a wine
glass in his yellow fingers. The grandees of criticism

had been assembled—Mayo Hazeltine, probably the
most powerful reviewer of the decade and Marrion
Wilcox who was concluding an attempt to get facts
from the war's beginning legend and soon rather
shocked the world by his history's impartial discussion of the Spanish side.   The luncheon was a failure and Crane fell asleep on a couch in his admirer's
house that afternoon without apology.   He was
twenty-seven and had given up adding a year to his
age while Howells was amused by his references to
"my youth" and, "when I was young."   In the operation of his mind, he was now an elderly, settled
character of many responsibilities who needed a
house in the country and had thoughts of buying a
ranch in Texas.   Once sensitively keen to hear what
people were saying about his work, it left him cool
to know that President McKinley had spoken favourably of "The Little Regiment."   But the President
had been a soldier.   "He would know if the stuff was
real or not, even," Crane drawled, "if he can't write
good English."

On November 23rd, he strolled into Delmonico's
bar with Huneker and the critic nodded to Thomas
McCumber who was idle at a table.   The pair drank
cocktails and went off to dine somewhere, at the
Everett House or in some German restaurant where
talk might be unbridled and the frothing outpour
of Huneker's conversation need not shock ladies.
But at Delmonico's tongues were busy.   Somebody

knew Crane by sight and a discussion began. Was
it true that he'd tried to get himself killed in Cuba?
McCumber pulled himself into the chatter, uninvited.
It was true, he said. Some incredulous stranger
argued the point. Why should a famous young
writer try to kill himself? The gigantic photographer grew noisy and men coming in for dinner
stopped to listen. Crane was dying of nameless and
disgusting diseases and everybody knew it. A reporter protested and the giant wanted to fight him.
Richard Harding Davis had come in alone and was
quietly ordering dinner in a corner of the room. After a moment he shouldered through the fringe at
the bar and commanded McCumber to be still. Mc-
Cumber didn't obey. He repeated his indictment
with additions, towering and swaying above Davis's
evening dress while an alarmed waiter pulled at his
coat. The smaller man wearied and twenty or
thirty people were witnesses of a suppression by
force. Davis, blushing furiously, towed the big
gossip out of the place and came back with his cus-
tomary dignity and a cut lip to ask such men as he
knew to forget the affair. . . . All penalties of the
popular writer have now been paid by Davis. A
general damnation has included his alert sketches of
London and Paris and the satiric portrait of "Captain
Macklin," the military cad. The mind displayed
was, perhaps, conventional but the man had a persisting quality most remarkable. He would praise and

advertise his rivals and his betters with pen and voice. He lauded his successor, Gouverneur Morris, and distributed the first book of James Huneker to friends who didn't want to read it and could not understand what it meant. He called attention to Crane's reports of the Cuban war and afterwards, when he was obliged to explain who Crane had been, spent hours in description of the man who always, clearly, somehow shocked and puzzled him. Crane was "a strange genius" but that genius should not be neglected. This oddity of temperament got him into trouble when Stanford White was murdered by some inconsequent fellow in a quarrel over a trumpery woman who then was shown at the trial tricked out as a schoolgirl. The legal proceedings were so cynical in their appeal that the New York press recorded them with real unwillingness. The dead architect's mild sensualities were sprayed with slime so completely that the reviving courage of his friends has not yet established the hollowness of the attack. Here and there journalists and writers feebly denied that White was Nero recrudescent. He was a jolly, harmless pagan who possessed an enormous enthusiasm for art, art in all kinds. He was now reviled by men who had dined at his expense the week before his death and artists fled from the remains of their patron with that speed begotten in cowards by a scandal involving lust. Davis was not intimate with the monster but this strange sense of

justice flashed out in a published praise of White.
The man had been kind, talented and generous,
slain by a drunken fool. The brave reporter shouted
against the world his outraged theory of fair play
and his books were forthwith dumped from a public
library in New Jersey while lads were warned by
the headmaster of a famous school to beware "Soldiers of Fortune" and "The Princess Aline" as foul
emanations of a depraved romancer. Only in an
English-speaking country was such a folly possible
and only an American could know the consequences
of the act. It leaves him lonely in the tale of the
national letters.

2

The alliance of Crane and James Huneker began
casually and without much warmth on Crane's part
but in the autumn of 1898 they walked and dined
together frequently. A change was apparent in
Crane. . . . His earlier friends were scattering. Cor-
win Linson went abroad in October and John Willard
Raught, another young painter, was gone too. John
Northern Hilliard had become an editor in Rochester.
Hamlin Garland was much in the west and Edward
Townsend was often travelling. The men of the
Lantern Club were bully fellows and he could en-
tertain himself with the garrulous wit of Acton
Davies, but discontent had set in and he found him-
self thinking of England while he hunted a house

in New York. Lounging at tea with a lady in December this came to expression. "Englishmen aren't shocked as easily as we are. You can have an idea in England without being sent to court for it."

His ideas and opinions had not given Edward Garnett, Harold Frederic or Ford Maddox Hueffer any moments of uneasiness. He sometimes appalled Robert Barr who was conservatively minded but Stephen Crane's cynicisms have by this year paled into common sense. His objection to the Mosaic deity, of course, did not belong to his decade of careful avoidance. It is known that he startled by an aristocratic habit of calling peasants in America, peasants. He derided the sacred petting of all Irishmen. His description of pity as "a virtue almost useless in ninety-nine cases out of a hundred. . . ." seemed affectation in 1896. His political thinking is obscured but the violence of his rages with social and religious limitation is recalled. He had no patience with doctrines that sank individuals into the mass and defined their mental path. "Frances Willard," he told Miss Harris, "is one of those wonderful people who can tell right from wrong for everybody from the polar cap to the equator. Perhaps it never struck her that people differ from her. I have loved myself passionately now and then but Miss Willard's affair with Miss Willard should be stopped by the police." At some time he "was a Socialist for two weeks but when a couple of Socialists assured me I

had no right to think differently from any other Socialist and then quarrelled with each other about
what Socialism meant, I ran away."

His views on women alarmed some of his friends.
Against the current of the '90s he was both chivalrous
and realistic. He had got himself in jail by protect-
ing a streetwalker from a bullying policeman but
"most streetwalkers would be 'demimondianes' "—so
spelled—"if they had money. Lots of women are
just naturally unchaste and all you jays know it,"
yet the faint tinge of Puritanism lay in him. He
was perpetually nervous when gentlewomen smoked
before him and a man who would accept a woman's
prolonged fidelity without offering her marriage was,
in some way not explained, censorable. He projected
in "The Monster" and "Active Service" finely compressed sketches of disagreeable middle-aged women,
but a pretty girl was too much for his detachment
and only a frantic admirer would join Elbert Hubbard in calling Crane a profound student of the female mind. The heiress of "The Third Violet" takes
on rank life when she throws herself at the head of
the timid, obtuse Hawker but elsewhere, like the
novel, she is something never quite finished. There
was no androgynous streak in Crane and perhaps
without that embarrassing trace no man writes well
of women until age has calloused him to the wonder
of a body unlike his own. However, some of his random annotations were disliked and he lightly ex-

pressed rather unusual thoughts, for his time. It
was not circumspect in an American to suggest that
women knew "the joys of cruelty." Margharita and
her mother in "The Clan of No Name" were too
frank for many readers. He once wrote the story of
an artist's model who married into a small town but
the tale froze editors while it amused James
Huneker and it has disappeared.

Crane was lingering, hesitant, with sour comment
reaching him as to his habits and customs. "There
must," said Huneker, "have been people who hated
the boy monumentally. Three or four times when
he had been spending the whole evening with Ryder
and myself I would be told in the morning how drunk
and disorderly he had been the night before by men
who had not seen him. For a mild and melancholy
kid he certainly had fallen completely into the gar-
bage can of gossip. . . . The charm of his talk de-
fies description. It was all adjectives and adverbs.
He spoke of his friend Conrad as the devout speak
of the B. V. M. Harold Frederic's case was drag-
ging through the papers still and the bourgeois in
Park Row used to bore Crane about it a good deal.
He was a great individualist and he resented the
twaddle about suicide intensely as he knew that
Frederic could not have recovered anyhow. I saw
him last about Christmas time. . . ." After Christmas he reached decision suddenly. He would go
back to England and stay there. So he rode on the

frosty highways around Hartwood with his brother
and once his horse fell with him at a turn.   Then he
sailed on the *Manitou* in the first week of January. . . . Perhaps with some regrets.   That New
York, that acreage of brown stone and shoddy stucco
was altering and imperial tones of marble shone
everywhere as hotel after hotel opened to dazzle
rustics with frescos and satin chairs.   Little pleasures
faded in the crash of new display but he might recall long breakfasts in hot summer under the striped
awning of the Vienna Bakery beside white Grace
Church and the wet bodies of prizefighters lurching
in the smoke of Harry Hill's queer restaurant where
lightweights fought while men dined. . . . Music of
that decade was the rolling of hansoms and he who
so loved shimmering tones of light might remember
the damp sheen of cabs on Broadway.   There had
been the young talk of the Hotel Griffon and the
Bœuf a la Mode and the fresh voice of the Wild
Indians in their barrack on Twenty Third Street.
He would not forget a murmurous park with a pair
of white arms beside him as he was driven around
and around through warm night and in an alien
valley he would be sick again for the sight of tall
towers and the noise of hurrying wheels.

VIII

THE LAST

WRITING to Edward Garnett on January 10, 1899, Cora Crane showed a knowledge of her husband's situation in two sentences: "His great difficulty is a lack of that machine-like application which makes a man work steadily. I hope that the perfect quiet of Brede Place and the freedom from a lot of dear good people, who take his mind from his work, will let him show the world a book that will live. . . ." Nine men, breathing or extinct, have claimed that they first mentioned Brede to Stephen Crane but to Mr. Garnett belongs the credit of a sensible suggestion made in November of 1897. The critic advised Crane to find a house somewhere less easy of access. He talked of Brede as an available ruin and Mrs. Crane went to investigate while Crane enjoyed Cuba. So, on January 16th, they drove from Hastings through twilight and Crane saw his next home by the pleasing glow of lamps. The house, begun in the fourteenth century, was wonderfully dilapidated and an owl had built a nest on a beam of the panelled hall. He was charmed by the faint sound of water spilling under the bridge and by his wife's delight in this solidified romance: "It is a pretty fine affair," he wrote to Sanford Bennett, "and Cora believes that Sir Walter Scott designed it for her. They began one wing in 1378 and somebody kidded it with heavy artillery in Cromwell's time. We shall move in as soon as we can. I enclose 10 pounds. Do I owe you more than that?"

Brede was a relief after Oxted and Crane's stored goods were sent from Hartwood. Mexican blankets hung red and white on the walls of a little room above the gateway and furniture was somehow bought for ten chambers. The butler, Heather, appeared and undertook by stern discomposures to correct his master's habit of running downstairs coatless to meet guests. Maurice Hewlett was shocked on calling to find Crane in muddy boots when the ride that excused such articles had been taken before breakfast. Henry James came from Rye to inspect and was pained to hear Sanford Bennett call Crane, "Baron Brede." An abrasion of tradition and privilege had occurred by no known intention. To Crane his manor was a playhouse and to some of his friends —or acquaintances—it was a sanctity invaded, carelessly, by an irreverent whose claret they would gladly still consume while they sighed in London over his bad form. A literary clergyman arriving to ask a hundred signed copies of "Bowery Tales"

in the name of a charitable bazaar was peculiarly
outraged by the sight of Crane in a grey flannel shirt
rolling dice with strange adjurations on the hall's depressed floor. It is recorded that these dice were "not
of the ordinary colour and must be American," and
that, at tea, there were small, flat "hot rolls which
Mrs. Crane insistently called biscuit although they
were not biscuit but agreeable." Oh, England!

Crane worked and "the dear, good people" did not
get at him unless they were summoned. He was
reading a great deal. His individuality did not regard itself as a completed labour of God, at twenty-
seven, and chance had dropped him among critical
folk who knew things. His reverence, when one
finds the quality coming to view, was latterly on the
drift away from men who could do things and ex-
pending itself on men who knew things, on Huneker
and on the Garnetts whose progenitor "bossed the
British Museum and talked about old man Caxton
as if they had been at school together." The advantage of a little pedantry had been pointed out to
Crane by Ripley Hitchcock and by Hamlin Garland
whose books he borrowed and probably never returned since his one absolute vice was a habit of not
sending books back. He returned money when he
thought of it with long apologies for his remissness
but books he simply took and kept. So in one week
of March, 1899, he read a volume on Greek vases,
Turgenev's "Smoke," Du Maurier's "Peter Ibbetson,"

—(he didn't like it)—"Cashel Byron's Profession,"
"Literature and Dogma," "In the Cage," presented
to him by Henry James with an elaborate and almost
affectionate inscription, in French. History, save
as the background of battles, he had never much ex-
plored until now and its fascination was plain in
Sussex with walls so ancient shedding dampness on
him and the ghost of William the Conqueror
troubling his wife's dreams. He even read May's
constitutional history of England and survived without trouble the involuted dreariness of its manner.
Huneker still wanted him to read Balzac but Mr.
Conrad had told him all about Balzac and he held
himself excused.

With spring Brede was gayer. He had pledged a
series of articles on great battles and fancied he
would enjoy the work. *Harper's Magazine* wanted
him to continue the stories of Whilomville. "Active
Service" was finished and in print. Half a dozen
tales had been sold and he could cheerfully lend a
hundred pounds without taking a note. So he saw
more people and the butler hired more servants to
support his dignity properly. In April Crane discovered several housemaids washing the battalion
of dogs necessary to life and wondered at Heather's
ability. "My man," he wrote, "can hire me a pair
of maids while I ride to Rye and back. If I went
to Russia I should come home and find Parliament
in buttons and Marie Corelli in the kitchen." But

the maids were useful to wash Sponge and his con-
sort Flannel and the solemn Russian poodles who
were so indiscreet when they called on Henry James
at Rye. Young ladies played absurd games in the
hall with young authors after dinner and Crane
watched nascent flirtations devotedly, although his
wife refused him lamps with red shades.

He had come under scientific eyes and Mark Barr [1]
caught his passion for red. The walls of the study
must be made soothing by paint of a shade between
vermillion and claret, the colour of fresh sumach on
the hills around Port Jervis. This red meant comfort, thrilling excitement or desire according to the
mood. When some eventual psychologist has
cleared from the investigation of such manias
the guesses now clinging to them, Crane's work will
be a chart of illustration. Writers in all degrees
have indulged in favourite colours. Greys and soft
blues abound in the stanzas of Verlaine. Henry
James had a positive, but not crude, affection for
clean floods of light and for brown dusks of interior.
William Morris would halt an address to stare at certain shades of orange or dull green, a woman once
noticed, and resume Socialism when some memory
was slaked in his brain. In Crane's work one sees
milder manias. Purple was sinister and repugnant.
Greyish blue and strong yellow were pleasant.
Above everything comes the notice of lamps seen in

[1] Mr. Barr is an American chemist.

the dark. . . . "Down an alley there were sombre curtains of purple and black, on which the street lamps dully glittered like embroidered flowers. . . ." When Mrs. Chaffee played for him some phrases of Debussy the swift notes were . . . "windows in a train at night going over the edge of a plain. . . ." A kindness of Moreton Frewen was "a searchlight on a hungry boat at sea. . . ." and the foolish, persisting air whistled by American troops in Cuba was "a jumble of Chinese lanterns in a fog." Half Crane's achievement in letters was his astonishing ease of visual description and seemingly simple statements have a haunting effect of complete justice to a scene. Nothing could be better than the two lights of "The Open Boat" which were the "furniture of the world," to his racked eyes.

"The Open Boat" appeared in the autumn of 1898 and American critics received these tales with the calm cordiality and the lack of criticism that maddens. One review alone rises from the banal level of the list. Rupert Hughes wrote of the new book with a sensitive appreciation and a considerable analysis of the methods employed. The other reviews were kind and flat. Crane exploded in a fluff of angry words before the sympathetic Edward Garnett. Some day he might make Americans forget "The Red Badge"! He wanted to know what certain American reviewers would have to say, in the next year, of "The Blue

Hotel" but nobody said anything very discriminating and Mark Twain thought it a grisly business. The Lincoln of our letters was never pleased by grimness in the fiction of other writers and Crane, told of this censure, simply grinned.

American failure to recognize Crane's short stories was not so sweeping as it may have seemed to him. His nation's tribute to Crane has been the compliment of conscious or unconscious theft and if only the inferior wartime episodes of "The Little Regiment" were broadly popular, "The Blue Hotel," "Death and the Child," "A Desertion" and "The Five White Mice" have been much honoured in a ghostly fashion. He swayed clean from the national orbit. Where Ambrose Bierce failed by clinging to the tradition of Poe, Crane failed by a blank abandonment of the form still sacred with editors and critics, the truncated novel produced by Harte and De Maupassant. He was interested to sketch curtly coloured crossroads on the map of existence and that map had for him no sure or solacing pattern. His vision of the world is jabbed into "The Blue Hotel" by a symbol atrocious to the soft and, one supposes, distressing to the pious. A panicky and tipsy Swede is knifed in a Nebraskan saloon by a mild little gambler who, in Crane's speech, is merely the apex of a human movement, an adverb in the meaningless sentence. But the corpse of the Swede, "alone in the saloon, had its eyes fixed upon a dreadful legend that dwelt atop the cash-machine: 'This registers the amount of your purchase'. . . ." and Crane, indifferent to his childish public, did not stop to brandish paragraphs of comment on the futility of such a bargain. Thus in "Wise Men" the two charming Kids back a fat old bartender against a trained runner in a footrace, for no reason, and their champion wins. Accident dominates an inchoate society. In the weaker "Twelve O'Clock" an idle argument about a cuckoo clock brings death on two men and the cuckoo pokes out its inhuman head to squawk twelve times over the heaped slaughter. Once it begins, this human movement proceeds with all the vigour of a holy war but there is no cause to justify the hopes and terrors, the pompous stir of man's nonsensical activity under nature's bland survey. Rewards are as accidental as calamities. In "Active Service" the war-correspondent gets his sweetheart by merit of being the chance rescuer of her parents and through no virtue whatever. In "The Clan of No-Name," one of Crane's poorest efforts, one still sees the dull Mr. Smith win Margharita simply because her lover is dead under the machete in Cuba. Even in "The Red Badge of Courage" the boy is allowed his moment of glory as the army staggers off the field in retreat. It needs no critical power to know that this perpetual refutation of endeavour is a thing disconcerting to the general, a caviare of pebbles. Edgar Saltus, setting forth in a polished and most literary style his derived philosophy of negations was a figure more comfortable to the times, especially as he piled such a treasure of lewd facts in the lives of Czars and rowdy, luxurious Cæsars, a treat to housewives and that sort of critic for whom art is not art unless the toys of art be shown. Add to Crane's matter, the manner described by Richard Gilder—privately—as grim flippancy and the reason of his failure is plain enough. In "The Bride Comes to Yellow Sky," his own favourite, he shows the drunken Wilson lurching through streets of barred and silent houses, death in his hand, then makes the man absurd in the universe by mention of his shirt from a Bowery sweat shop and of his boots with the red tops dear to little boys in snowy winter. He forbids primitive emotional relish to break out. The adobe house scarred by the cowboy's bullets rebukes his magnificence with its immobile dignity. The town is Wilson's plaything but he, threshing his revolvers, is the plaything of a sardonic, casual fortune. Man is just man, even in the hour of courage when Crane lets him be, homely and awkward still, an image of endurance not without honour, not, in the end, without beauty. It should be remembered that in his decade's critical vocabulary "ironic" was a reproachful adjective.

One Cuban night Acton Davies [1] was moaning for

---

[1] This is directly quoted from a letter of Mr. Davies dated July 2nd, 1898. The story was at once twisted to suit the

his dear Broadway.   He wanted such and such dishes
at his pet restaurant, such wines and a lustrous lady
to sit across from him.   Crane cut short the dream
by saying, "Why don't you just say you want a good
meal and a girl and be done with it?"   That salvage,
somewhat brutal, of the real from the sentimental
obliquity was the right token of Crane's offence
against the spirit of his day.

Brede Place warmed and Crane wrote through silent nights, lying abed until noon.   Harold Frederic's
lovely orphans played on the lawn and bruised their
fingers in the old falconry.   Mrs. Richie, from Ken-
tucky, and her handsome daughters were privileged
guests.   Robert Barr, H. G. Wells, A. E. W. Mason
came and went.   England was mildly concerned with
the Boers but Crane heard that three regiments and
some cavalry would chasten these yokels.   This
prophecy was made at Rye while Mrs. Humphry
Ward poured tea for Henry James.   Crane thought
the lady pleasant but duller than a President and he
had doubts as to the Boers.   "People tell me that
the South Africans and the Japanese can shoot like
the devil and then tell me a couple of Guard regiments could whip them in a week.   When a Yankee
says such things he is bragging but I guess an Eng-

mythology of Stephen Crane and has been printed as Crane's
statement, "If I were on Broadway tonight all I'd want would
be a bottle of whiskey and a woman." I regret the obligations
of veracity in spoiling so neat an epigram.

lishman is just lugging the truth from some dark cave."

A party escorted his niece Helen to Paris and there waited while Crane took the girl on to her school at Lausanne. Money still passed through his fingers without stopping and he had to borrow to get back to Paris. But now he was scared and working furiously: his wife must be secured for the future. He must try to repay his brothers the loans they had never mentioned. He would not live beyond thirty-one, he thought, and serenely drawled that guess to Karl Harriman when Robert Barr brought the young American down to Brede. "I never thought I'd live long," he said, "and I'm not much account any more." The mental tensity that had supported his first writing now was gone with health. Everything relaxed. He still rode Hengist or Horsa at a gallop along lanes and carried pots to the flower show where Henry James helped Edith Richie to sell love potions in a booth and enchanted Crane by a sentence that had easily thirty clauses and nine parentheses. He sometimes drove the trap whose wheels were painted in the sombre colours of the Crane armour—although he wouldn't explain the choice when he was asked. Pride of race was one of his secrets and he shrank from snobbery as he shrank from talk of his health. . . . What did he think of death? With Robert Barr he had wasted a night in burlesque incantations to bring Harold Frederic back and, Barr wrote, "Stephen put me to bed about dawn but we did not evoke anything except one of his dogs." Brooding suited him less than did endless discussions of everything in the stone kitchen while July storms showed wet haycocks on the slope by flares of lightning and Mr. Mason's eyeglass was a violet round to catch his stare. Death? Here was humanity. Why bother? And he could dash off a tale about a haycock just to show Barr and Harriman how the thing was done.

His manners were not silken but he had always inoffensively gone through proper parties in New York or London. Lady Randolph Churchill thought him somewhat formal and other hostesses were surprised to hear that Crane was in any way Bohemian. He could be diplomatic when he chose; one of his guests recalls the nimbleness with which Crane manipulated conversations to spare the feelings of a man lately divorced. His natural informality was not a parade of what is called the artist's freedom as in England he found himself more at ease among intelligences than in America: "I once horrified Elbert Hubbard and his household by telling the story of an old negress in Minetta Lane I met when I was working for Ed Marshall on the *Press*. This old black devil was taking a bath in a wash-boiler when I walked into her flat and she called, 'Chile, I'se all disdressed.' That anecdote slew its thousands at Hubbard's and got me in much trouble. I shall never know why. They acted as though I had read one of Zola's loudest roars. Over here I have told it in front of seven or eight mothers of families and I assure you nothing happened. Nothing at all." He told the anecdote to Maurice Hewlett who responded, "Ah? She meant that she was distressed? I see," and the response possibly explains why no friendship ripened between Crane and the author of "Richard Yea and Nay."

Crane liked people for obscure reasons and his open dislikes were so few that inevitably he collected both bores and boors. In moments of frightful tedium he occasionally rounded on some one with jibes too subtle for thick skins. A journalist appeared at Brede and paralysed all present by his overbearing rudeness for three days. On the fourth morning he lodged a complaint about a servant who hadn't brought something to his room and Crane drawled, "Perhaps she has patrician instincts," but the journalist stayed on until through James Pinker, Mrs. Crane managed to dismiss him. Once in July Crane broke out to his literary agent, "If you don't tell some of these lice that Cora and I aren't running a hotel I'll have to advertise the fact in the *Times!*" and then cleared his dwelling by taking off five youngsters to the Henley regatta. "How," he asked Sanford Bennett, "does it come to pass that anybody in England thinks he can come and stay with me before I've asked him and patronize my wife's housekeeping?" He wrote to Elbert Hubbard: "I must have Egyptian blood in me. Mummies rise from the tomb and come to pay me calls that last for days."

Summer was pleasant, though, and he got slowly through the Whilomville series but finding that the Great Battles wearied him simply finished them off as he could in dry recitals of fact not anywhere florid but never enriched. One or two of the histories—such as Bunker Hill—have an interest but nothing went well with Crane when he wrenched his talent from its bent. In "Active Service" he had attempted a popular novel and had failed as he failed in popular reporting. The story lacks all the devices of its brand. Crane could not take his journalist seriously either in his professional aspect or as a lover. Fitfully the book glows—the lights of Broadway are jewels of a giantess, the poker game is a real game, the moment when the correspondent wanders in darkness beyond the Greek lines is wonderfully rendered, but "Active Service" dropped far below Crane's standard and some of his friends were indignant for the contemptuous portrait of a newspaperman. Some wrote to him their outrage with the poem in "War is Kind" when the verses were printed.

> "A newspaper is a court
> Where every one is kindly and unfairly tried
> By a squalor of honest men.
> A newspaper is a market

Where wisdom sells its freedom
And melons are crowned by the crowd. . . ."

"A newspaper is a symbol;
It is fetless life's chronicle,
A collection of loud tales
Concentrating eternal stupidities,
That in remote ages lived unhaltered,
Roaming through a fenceless world."

The grey book of poems again bewildered reviewers. He was still writing unrhymed lines and his
sentiments were still unusual. The first poem was
somehow cryptic, or silly. They were not sure.
"Mr. Crane's sense of humour," a Bostonian had to
say, "is of a mystifying kind. He deliberately shows
us the horrors of war and then entitles his work 'War
is Kind.'" It wouldn't do.

"Do not weep, maiden, for war is kind.
Because your lover threw wild hands towards the sky
And the affrighted steed ran on alone,
Do not weep.
War is kind.
Hoarse, booming drums of the regiment,
Little souls who thirst for fight,
These men were born to drill and die.
The unexplained glory flies above them,
Great is the battle-god, great, and his kingdom—
A field where a thousand corpses lie. . . ."

All the best poems of this second attack on formal
versification are known to date from 1895, 1896 and

1897.   Several were written while Crane and Captain Murphy lamented the *Commodore* in Jacksonville. Some experiments in rhythm go along excellently but the love poems are not fired by the spirit of the earlier work and only here and there is the tone of amusement memorable.

> " 'Have you ever made a just man?'
>   'Oh, I have made three,' answered God,
>   'But two of them are dead,
>   And the third—
>   Listen! Listen!
>   And you will hear the thud of his defeat.' "

> "A man said to the universe:
>   'Sir, I exist.'
>   'However,' replied the universe,
>   'The fact has not created in me
>   A sense of obligation.' "

Very plainly rises his own patrician instinct before the spectacle of some triumphant vulgarian in a nest of spoils once the goods of better men.

> " . . . The outcry of old beauty
>   Whored by pimping merchants
>   To submission before wine and chatter. . . ."

If anything is to be gained by analysis of "War is Kind," the book shows less agitation.   The man of 1898 has got done with musing on sexual adventure as "sin" and his young quarrel with a Jewish tribal

divinity is over.   Sin had become for Crane any act
of disloyalty to the given purpose.   "Men have never
much deserved Christ and Buddha," he wrote, "because they went to work and changed the teaching
of generosity into a teaching of roars and threats.
I can not be shown that God bends on us any defin-
able stare, like a sergeant at muster, and his laughter
would be bully to hear out in nothingness."   As for
his theory of love, one sees in the verses a knowledge
of sentimentalized desire as a tumult not in proportion to the cause.   He was an amorist and young.
The interest was enormous, candid and not complex.
One thinks of him as a thoroughly romantic lover
who had not made many exactions in love and probably knew precious little of women.   He could finely
record the duel between the stupid George and his
narrow, devoted mother, because he could coarsen
his own figure and that of his parent, making Mary
Crane a scolding woman of the tenements and himself a dull young workman but the duel of desire was
too tremulously moving for discernment and his
erotic verse drops into the banal.

3

Crane seldom brought forth an opinion of a con-
temporary unless he was sure of his hearers but
sometimes he was driven to expression and often he
gave offence.   The man was generous, almost crazily
generous in his judgment up to a point, then out

poured his distaste for the dramatized personality and those minor arts of exhibition so dear to most writers. Luckless in all things he chose to say "an author is a man licensed by public opinion to act like a chorus girl at supper," when he was leaving the Savage Club after an evening with Mark Twain wooing adoration in the foreground. The retirement of Thomas Hardy struck him as "all right" and Mr. Kipling's notable absence from the drawing rooms was "the man's own business." These views were harmless but, and before the wrong audience, he drawled that he could write in a circle all around Marriott Watson. Vastly pleased by the startling "McTeague" of Frank Norris he yet pronounced the book too moral and that sensible objection was whispered along as proof of his conceit. He also said there was too much "I" in W. E. Henley's "Invictus" and preferred the poet's less popular stanzas.

He was conceited in streaks. An eminent writer who is proud of mastering the revolver and publicly wishes he could write verse as well as he plays poker—(Mr. William Crane denies that his brother could play poker even reasonably well)—is courting comment. Now and then fits of pride came on Crane and in one of these he announced that "The Bride Comes to Yellow Sky" was a whole heap better than anybody had said in print. Sometimes he seemed to be drinking in flatteries from very trivial people and then he was coolly indifferent to pleasant

words from beings in critical place. An air of ingratitude blew often in his drawl. His independence
was dear to Crane and he exploded in August of 1899,
"It seems that I am the only person who had nothing
to do with bringing myself before the public!" Indeed, on his side of the question, it should be said
that too many gentlemen of the late '90s had
"brought Stephen Crane before the public" and the
manner of that production remains hopelessly dark
after long investigation. He wrote: "I am, I think,
sufficiently grateful to men who really did things
for me and in particular to Mr. Garland who, as you
know, gave me sound advice about 'The Red Badge.'
But just what is it to the credit of A . . . and
B . . . that they bought things from me? I mean,
what is my obligation to them? They saw a profit
to their papers in buying my stuff and we break even.
If it comes to that sultry point, why shouldn't they
be grateful to me?"

But the ingratitude of authors to publishers,
critics and editors is a notorious thing and safety
lies in letting the balance tilt toward the apprais-
ing power. Crane further erred in writing, "Why
should I be grateful for an utterly bad piece of criticism that leaves out everything good in 'George's
Mother' and mentions just the things I would like to
write over again if that was honest?"

He would not re-write. He was careless in reading proof and for some of his books he never read

proof at all. Ripley Hitchcock begged him to think over "The Third Violet" as Crane admitted many scenes were too compressed but the story had appeared as a serial and it was "dishonest" to change the thing now that it had been offered to readers. He restored only a few paragraphs of "The Red Badge" for its final form, so an opening description of the two armies as watchful beasts which so pleased Mr. Garland is for ever lost. Sketches dashed off in a few hours were issued with all their imperfections just as first seen in *The Press* and *The World*. Enormous holes appear in his egotism and his failure in grooming himself for the general gaze is a thing too curious.

"A little ink more or less!
    It surely can't matter?
Even the sky and the opulent sea,
The plains and the hills, aloof,
    Hear the uproar of all these books.
    But it is only a little ink more or less."

People came to Brede Place in the autumn of 1899 in numbers fatally large for the bank account. An insurrection occurred one morning in September and the household was cut down. By strenuous devices Crane swept the manor for a visit of Mr. and Mrs. Conrad and then was overwhelmed with guests invited or self invited in the month's last week. Certain friends had license to come and go as they

pleased. He was always glad to see Mrs. Richie and
her daughters, Robert Barr, Mark Barr, H. G. Wells
and A. E. W. Mason. He wrote, "John Stokes and
George Lynch have the kindness to let Cora know
when they are coming but would to God that some
of the other Indians would write and ask." . . . A
paradox established itself. To some of his English
friends Brede seemed a Bohemian stronghold while
roaming Americans thought Stephen Crane in severe
evening dress surrounded by formal gowns and black
coats a most unhallowed spectacle, the Bohemian
turned snob. Mark Barr suggested that hollows of
the hall's flooring had once been filled with rushes
and for a week or so rushes littered the place, painfully impressing Henry James as a parody of baronial
state. A village blacksmith hammered iron holders
for candles and the beams had their ancient light
again. Its ghosts were invited back to Brede and
its master of the moment, reading the Whilomville
tales aloud to his young circle coughed gently as
mists of October leaked through his ruinous dwelling
in the most romantic way. Processions of dogs
followed him when he rode Hengist or drove Horsa
off to Rye and the white Powder Puff got her tail
caught under a door, on Crane's birthday. An off-
spring of Sponge and Flannel was selected for the use
of Master Borys Conrad and the Russian poodles
shed gloom by their presence at teas when literary ladies came to ask questions about Crane's

ethics. . . . All this went on while Mr. Conrad and Mr. Garnett were wondering about the gaunt man's lungs and his wife spent afternoons guarding his privacy in the red study. He had read with appreciation Knut Hamsun's "Hunger" when Karl Harriman brought the book to Brede in summer but appetite ceased and Mrs. Crane had agitated conferences with friends as to Switzerland and the Black Forest. He would not see doctors although he smoked less and less. Miss Edith Richie carefully poured doses of Scotch whiskey into a sea of soda and is still indignant: "Cora and I would mix his highballs for Stephen. There would be about a tablespoonful of Scotch at the bottom of the glass and I have heard men who were drinking five times as much say, 'He is drinking himself to death.' He would light a cigarette and then let it go out in his fingers and, when he noticed that, light another and men said, 'He is smoking too much. . . .' " He sat so with that faintly coloured beverage turning in his hand and listened to random talk. Now and then a rocket of adjectives mounted but he was becoming very silent and his voice went slowly while he praised the new Western sketches of Owen Wister and Alfred Henry Lewis.

He could still be excited by a discovery. Somebody urged him to read Anatole France and he went mad over "The Procurator of Judæa," that picture of the aged Pilate trying to remember any such

person as Jesus of Nazareth. He detailed his high
opinion of M. France to Henry James and to Edmund Gosse quite as though they had never heard
of the Frenchman. He besought William Heinemann to buy the next novel of Frank Norris. Un-
literary in his conduct Crane was yet a man of letters
although he chattered slang when talk became too
exquisite of an evening at the Savage or in the waste
spaces of the Reform Club. He had even critical
views a little prophetic: "I should say that Mr.
Wells will write better and better when he sticks to
characters altogether and does not so much concern
himself with narrative. I may be wrong but it seems
to me that he has a genius for writing of underclass
people more honestly than Charles Dickens. . . . I
will bet all my marbles and my best top that Walter
Besant is forgotten in twenty years. . . . Every one
tells me that Mr. Stevenson was a fine fellow but
nothing on earth could move me to change my belief
that most of his work was insincere."

He would forgive all other crimes if a writer
seemed to him honest in his scheme and for that
reason he championed artists dead or living who
were never important. His generosity gushed on
half a dozen commonplace realists who "tried to
write honestly about things." They did not get very
far but they must care for their work and that was
the point of honour. Æsthetic must be the application of emotional weight and to Crane it was plain

enough that the arts were merely departments of the intelligent treasure in humanity. Once Mark Barr was talking of a research in higher mathematics and ended, "You see, I cared so much."

Crane broke out, "That's it, Mark! Now that you've said it always remember it. You can never do anything good æsthetically—and you can never do anything with anything that's any good except æsthetically—unless it has at one time meant something important to you."

In the same spirit he wrote to a youth who wasn't sure whether his genius would find better expression in sculpture or fiction: "You might be one of the people who have picked on a defenceless art as a means of telling how much certain things have meant, or mean to you, but did you ever think that this world is full of artists in alligator growing and the promulgation of mixed vegetables? Mr. James was recently quoting a piece from some French poet [1] who shows Narcissus seeing in himself the motion of all time. An artist, I think, is nothing but a powerful memory that can move itself at will through certain experiences sideways and every artist must be in some things powerless as a dead snake. Blessed in simile, did any writer ever limit the power of his vision by such a figure? Perhaps the secret of Crane's charm for many men lay in his rebuke of the artist's swollen vanity. He wrote to his intimate

[1] Obviously André Gide.

Hilliard. . . . "For I understand that a man is born into the world with his own pair of eyes, and he is not at all responsible for his vision—he is merely responsible for his quality of personal honesty. To keep close to this personal honesty is my supreme ambition. . . ."

Himself Crane recognized his lucklessness and lightly mentioned it to Willis Clarke when his admirer called at Brede in late November. Ripley Hitchcock had given the young fellow a note of introduction and Crane interrupted work to see him. Lamps were already lighted and Mr. Clarke's eye was caught by a photograph of Hall Caine framed on the wall with a legend below the familiar black cloak, "Christ on the Mountains of Man." Mr. Clarke wanted to write down their talk in shorthand and Crane was listlessly amused. He spoke of his parents at some length and then of "Maggie" but his attention veered. He began to ask questions about Texas and about baseball teams in the middle west. Mr. Clarke brought him round by saying, "It's hard luck that you and Mr. Kipling began to write at the same time."

"Yes. I'm just a dry twig on the edge of the bonfire," said Crane.

Chance had erected him as a slim, inscrutable statue before the running opal and fierce light of a talent then shimmering so changefully in the lettered air. It was just his luck.

4

Christmas must be gay. He was homesick. He filled Brede with youth and his wife cooked passionately. There were theatricals and the ghosts of Brede romped visibly. The dog Sponge became a father on New Year's Eve and Crane lifted his glass to the oncoming months with, "Let's drink to the Twentieth Century—in spite of your objection, Mark," he added to Mr. Barr who had scientifically assured him that the century was not yet begun on January 1, 1900. But they danced through the night and guests trailed up to the rooms of the turret where C. Lewis Hind and other hardy souls had to sleep on cots. A man came back for a forgotten cigarette case and saw Crane at one of his oddities, humming with his face close to the strings of a violin. His guest strolled up to speak to the dreamer and Crane fainted suddenly against his shoulder.

Alarm had commenced among his friends. Robert Barr was urging a voyage to South Africa in salt air. Some days after the New Year, Crane spoke of Texas to James Pinker. He had been very well down there and living was cheap. Moreton Frewen advised the south of France. People were not willing to say so, but they saw all signs of consumption. Crane listened to nothing and worked at highest speed, inviting folk to keep "Cora from seeing spooks." One night there was long poker and, next

afternoon, he led a party of unshaven friends to a
tavern in Rye where they idled under the stare of a
most civilized person in a shadowy corner. Crane recalled his errand in the town as dusk fell. He must
take back a manuscript to Henry James. The civilized being lifted from obscurity a voice of cultivated
distress. Mr. James would not see a stranger save on
appointment.

"Oh, sir," said Crane, "I know that the duel is not
practised in this country but I am prepared to waive
that for your benefit."

The votary faded out and Crane was commanded
to bring his friends into Lamb House where ladies
were dressed to dine. The Jamesian servants, so
dreaded by the master, brushed off tweed coats and
dinner went graciously forward. James played a
joke on a matron who denounced prizefights. He
had seen one, he said amid shudders, and slowly detailed the sweating muscles and the bestial faces of
the crowd, all viewed, it turned out, on the decent
screen of a crude moving picture show. . . . Sometimes he seems to have stared with a strange wistful-
ness across the parapet of his seclusion. He must
ask Mr. Hueffer's thoughts on the peasants about
Rye and he must hear from Crane how cowboys
lived and, if their livid emotion deserved that verb,
loved. A little later he would weary an ailing
millionaire at Hyères for the facts of his pauper boy-
hood. How did a person who so well knew French

happen to have been a farmhand at thirteen? How was it allowed? Was—er—was there no resource? No, no grandfather had flourished in the Illinois of his friend's childhood to dispense millions among a dozen descendants and make it certain that nobody need worry about money or have to know coarse and humble people. "Oh," said the novelist of the finer grain, "horrible! Damnable!" . . . What did he think of the tired guest at his table who had "lived with violence" and was "so truly gifted" and "so very lovable" and "had the mannerisms of a Mile End Roader" and "was of the most charming sensitiveness" in his somewhat diverse and troubled expressions? He sent to Stephen Crane, unasked, five manuscripts and invited an opinion, so he must have respected something in the weary impressionist. Being very old he said, "I loved him. . . ." and that, perhaps, was a convenient synthesis for a mind wanting to understand but not approving the vivid wayfarer.

On January 20th Crane drifted into Mr. Pinker's office and reclaimed two tales mailed the day before from Brede. They weren't good enough, he said. His agent asked how the New Year's party had gone and Crane drawled, "I've heard it was a Babylonian orgy."

A confused impression followed. People were told that Crane had shut Brede and was gone to New York or to the Continent and Robert Barr wrote, on

January 24th, to an American: "Mrs. Crane is so incensed by the nonsense talked about the New Year party at Brede that Stevie is taking her home. England has been kind to Stevie in many ways but some of his cherished friends have said things too carelessly about his most generous but not too formal hospitality and I have heard some gossip that must wound him deeply. His skin is very thin and he is subject to a kind of jealousy that knows how to hurt him worst. His present plan is to take some land in Texas and live in the open air but, between ourselves, it is all over with the boy. He may last two years but I can not bring myself to hope for more than that. . . . He sails on the first of the month." He did not sail. The mood lasted an evening after his explosion of disgust. Only a few people knew that he had thought of quitting England. The rumour started and died. He had begun a fantastic novel, "The O'Ruddy" and was sketching in the last sombre flood of his prose as "War Memories."

Meanwhile in America readers of *Harper's Magazine* were delighted and repelled by the Whilomville stories. For the first time since Mark Twain's demigod floated with his lazy slave on the Mississippi, the national child stepped forward and yelped among the maples and swinging gates of a little town, unmoral, unadorned and far from sweet. This creature lied and bragged and shocked ladies dreadfully. Crane's detachment wasted no loving words on Jimmie Trescott, Willie Dalzell and the petted daughter of the painter who blindly gave his brat five dollars and so desolated the land. Midway in the series is a pure tragedy. Jimmie took his share of picnic to the lake in a tin pail and all the children made him suffer for no reason. He was hooted and cast out because of this tin pail. It is the epic of democracies and Crane's enchantment with the idiocy of communal thought had its last fling. But the stories were not popular among mothers trained on Mrs. Burnett's patent food and male critics only were loud in praise. It was left for Booth Tarkington to prove the justice of Crane's performance and with gallantry to remind the public of his predecessor's exploit. Crane handles the children as he handled mature beings. There is the same gravity and the same lack of all respect for ordinary values. As usual not one adventure of Jimmie Trescott is a success. Everything turns out badly, down to the frustration of the Christmas Tree for whose glittering sake he joins an alien Sunday School. So biographical memory preserves soft female outcries against this cruel raid in the pink and white realm of childhood. . . . He had no luck at all. Surely in æsthetic mathematicians are most fortunate, raising their spells for the keen few in a tent of crystal fictions. Painters and makers of sounds have prompt appeal to a single sense and may thereby profit, but this written word must sink in a dark water of all senses mingled, rousing strange brutes of some forgotten dream, brushing to nervous life old prejudice submerged and shadowy in the mind that reads. Reward? No man of honour may demand felicity buttressed on ease in a world so subject to mere chance, but in the final dust vainglory can not thrill.

Friends wanted to send him as a correspondent for the *Morning Post* to Saint Helena but one day of March his mouth filled suddenly with blood while he petted a dog at luncheon and nobody had much hope, after doctors had shaken their heads. He rallied in April and was jubilant over the birth of twin nephews, one to be named Stephen Crane and destined to short life. People must come to Brede and amuse a frantic woman who paced the hall, trying to be affable still and bidding callers be sure to come again, reproaching herself for so much entertainment. Henry James, full of solicitudes, hurried to London when papers wrongly announced that Dr. Trudeau, the famous specialist of Saranac, was lodged in the city grown gloomy, as nothing went well with English armies in South Africa. Terrific fevers of the malady swept the man's fancy back to bright sands of New Jersey and he lay reading bits of his father's sermons. Once he was worried because Sanford Bennett recalled some words of Ford Hueffer and he sent after the Canadian a last note: "You must not be offended by Mr. Hueffer's manner. He patronizes Mr. James. He patronizes Mr. Conrad. Of course he patronizes me and he will patronize Almighty God when they meet but God will get used to it, for Hueffer is all right. . . ."

Robert Barr must finish "The O'Ruddy" and the Scotchman came to get orders for the jolly satire on old Ireland. Mrs. Crane thought of Germany after May entered Sussex and borrowed money broadcast for the useless journey. He was carried down to Dover and laughed when the dog Sponge clawed wallpaper in a room of the old Lord Warden. There Eugenie and the dead Prince Imperial had waited to welcome the last Napoleon into exile and being told so Crane stared at the Victorian adornments, whispering, "Hope she liked the carpet." Men came down out of a London surging with news of victories in South Africa. Ill himself Joseph Conrad dragged to Dover and watched the blue eyes rove to a sail that fled above grey water outside the window. Grace of indifference thickened. He did not care which world held him or if the multicoloured dice of a new being would flash beyond this towering shadow of the void. Out there? He didn't care, stroking his dog.

His niece joined him in hired chambers at Badenweiler and sun glowed in his wife's hair while he dictated orders for the gay novel and sometimes patted her white arms. On the fourth day of June he was very eager. Letters must go to his brothers and to

John Hilliard. Sponge hopped around the bed and must be teased for a while. Then it was night and the tired woman fell asleep, to be wakened before dawn by the little dog's vain howling in the dark.

THE END

APPENDIX

Stephen Crane is buried at Elizabeth, New Jersey, and a tablet to his memory is now in the Free Library of Newark. Mr. Max Herzberg of the Newark *Evening News* was one of the movers for this memorial and to Mr. Herzberg I am much indebted for the use of certain papers collected by him in his personal researches as to Crane. I must at once acknowledge an even greater indebtedness to Mr. Willis Clarke for his generosity toward me. In 1903 Mr. Clarke began to collect copies of letters and facts for a life of Stephen Crane but was so baffled by conflicting statements that he dropped the work. His shorthand report of an interview with Crane at Brede is quoted in Chapters 1, 3, and 4 and 7 of this book. He was also the donor of letters from Mrs. Bolton Chaffee, Julian Ralph, Robert Barr, Acton Davies and Henry Davies Hume, and of a passage in the diary of the late Charles Cary Griswold. The mythology encountered by Mr. Clarke may interest readers who have been struck by a note of apology in this most imperfect study. Mr. Clarke was informed by people who had met Crane and admired him that he was the illegitimate

243

son of Grover Cleveland, the outcast child of an eminent family in New York, an Australian sailor, a German actor and an ex-convict. He was gravely assured that the several published statements about Crane in journals, the *Bookman, Leslie's Weekly* and *Scribner's Magazine* were industrious camouflage devised by the late Ripley Hitchcock on behalf of Appleton's. My own contact with the legendary Crane revealed other jewels of rumour. I have, with regret, rejected the tales of Crane's love affair with the lamented Sarah Bernhardt, of his duel in New Orleans, of his attempt to burn James Gordon Bennett's yacht, of his marriage to Australian, English, Spanish and African dancers, of his ninety thousand dollar cablegram to the New York *Journal,* of his death of delirium tremens in Paris and of his murder by an actress still living who happened at the time of his death to be in Chicago. With less pain I have rejected anecdotes of Crane which were in print during his childhood as anecdotes of Mark Twain, Thomas Hood, Abraham Lincoln and Andrew Jackson. There have also been visited upon me stories of his gaieties which are, with probably as much truth, told in regard to Bill Nye, Eugene Field, Clyde Fitch and other celebrities still extant.

It was suggested to me by Mr. Huneker that Crane's picturesque exterior offered a field for the imagination of some contemporaries and that "they turned a little Flaubert into a big Verlaine." The

injustice of that romancing was great, however, and
inevitably I have concluded that a considerable spite
followed him after his success. Else why did three
unsigned letters reach me when Mr. Christopher
Morley printed my wish for correspondence in the
New York *Evening Post?* All three votaries of romantic biography had charges to make and the
charges were couched in excellent English.

Some of Crane's friends erred in their mention of
him after death. Elbert Hubbard's paper in *The
Philistine* contained equivocal statements and Robert
Barr's "qualities that lent themselves to misappre-
hension" is not a fortunate phrase. An article
printed as an obituary of Stephen Crane in a New
York paper of June 6th, 1900, took pains to clear him
of the charge of drug-taking and probably settled
that charge in the popular mind he so distrusted.
Three estimates likened him to Edgar Allan Poe
who is still, after scrupulous examination, held to
have been a drunken madman by the generality of
readers. Without doubt I shall be accused of "white-
washing" Crane and by choice I retort beforehand
that a man is entitled to his own identity, not to a
cheap shell of gossip. If my assumption that the
re-issue of "Maggie" roused silly conjectures is incorrect, it is in one instance well supported. Mr.
William Crane tells me that after "Maggie" appeared
in 1896 several ladies of Port Jervis solemnly con-
sulted him as to the propriety of receiving Stephen

Crane in their homes. . . . The American '90s present a singular mingling of poltroonery and bravado
in the treatment of sexual and alcoholic matters
public or private. You behold young men singing
Hovey's pretty "Stein Song" and you hear the last
despairing outcries of Frances Willard who wanted
her world to be Christian and in loud addresses assured it that Christ's kindness to the woman taken
in adultery was not an example to be imitated "in
our modern day." The author of "The Black Riders," "Maggie" and "George's Mother" was plainly
an object of suspicion and America never comes of
age. A fellow who defends streetwalkers in night
resorts and lends money to courtesans is naturally
"immoral." His intimates took Crane for a man of
honest and liberal views and their indignation with
the figure created for him by fiction persists. . . . I
take vast pleasure in issuing on behalf of a dead and
generous man a firm denial of an attack on Crane
in "The Derelict" by Richard Harding Davis.
Illustrations of the story happened to resemble Crane
somewhat and Mr. Davis suffered a deal of comment
for which he was not responsible.

This book is probably filled with errors but my
variations from partial biographies have been made
on the testimony of Crane's few letters. With
genuine regret I have differed from Mr. Hamlin Garland's account of the birth of "The Red Badge"
which, in his recollection, was first shown to him in

1893 and in the month of February. Crane's own
statement and the memory of other friends place the
writing rather later. I can only suggest that the
first rapid draft was the manuscript brought to Mr.
Garland in Harlem and that the finished product
was shown in the following winter. But Crane's
carelessness was astonishing. Belonging to the vain-
est of professions, he took no trouble to annotate
himself for history and that carelessness remains a
part of his charm for those who knew him. Many
of his last letters were written in a singular blue ink
that turned purple when dry and has now faded beyond process of revival. I have been unable to
verify Crane's career as a reporter on the *Herald*
and some amusing episodes have been omitted for
lack of proof. Also there have been removed from
his letters some hasty estimates of living people in
England and America. Crane himself had no great
idea of his judgment as to character on first sight as
he took Mr. George Bernard Shaw for a "clerical person" and Mr. Frank Harris for an actor. It would
have been pleasant to print his admiration of certain ladies who received him in England but the
wives of authors are entitled to such privacy as is
left in the world.

For their kindness in aiding me this book should
be dedicated to a number of people. If I have not
effected a portrait of the Stephen Crane known to
them, that is because, in his words, "an expression

of life can always elude us." Excuse me a little.
Another may do better. My thanks are offered,
among the unconcerned dead to: James Gibbons
Huneker, Charles Edward Devlin, Wallis McHarg,
Clyde Fitch, James Pinker, Acton Davies and to
Edmund Crane, among the living to William Howe
Crane, Edith Crane, Vera Sidmore, Hamlin Garland,
Mark Barr, Edith Richie Jones, Corwin Knapp Lin-
son, Frederic Gordon, Edward Garnett, Karl Edwin
Harriman, Vincent Starrett,[1] Paul Reynolds, Rich-
ard Brett Armstrong, Sarah McHarg, Victoria Sonn-
tag, John Langdon Heaton, Edward Sanford Bennett,
Charles Gardner 2nd, Claude Bragdon, Irving
Bacheller, Jesse Lynch Williams, Henry T. Carey,
John Northern Hilliard, John Willard Raught, Helen
Marie Campbell, Caroline Gunther, Eileen Bassett
Dufriche, Joseph and Jessie Conrad.

[1] Mr. Starrett's Bibliography contains all my information as to
Crane's unpublished work.